THE *UNCONVENTIONAL* COMPLIANCE OFFICER: DOING THINGS DIFFERENTLY

THE *SCIENCE* OF COMPLIANCE: *DRIVING YOUR PROGRAMME, REPUTATION & CAREER*

KEITH READ

THE UNCONVENTIONAL COMPLIANCE OFFICER: DOING THINGS DIFFERENTLY

©2022 McCormick Technologies Limited. All rights reserved

First edition published in Great Britain, 2022

This book or parts thereof may not be used or reproduced in any form, stored in any retrieval system or transmitted in any form by any means – electronic, mechanical, photocopy, recording or otherwise – without prior written permission of the publisher, except in the case of brief quotations embodied in articles and reviews. For information and permission requests, please contact the publisher at the address below.

The right of Keith Read to be identified as the author of this work has been asserted in accordance with the Copyright, Designs and Patents Act, 1988.

The author has made all reasonable efforts to contact copyright-holders for permissions, and apologies for any omissions or errors in the credits given. Corrections may be made in any future printings.

THE *UNCONVENTIONAL* COMPLIANCE OFFICER: DOING THINGS DIFFERENTLY

Contents

	Page
Foreword	9
A personal introduction: Compliance – *not Complacence*	13
How this book is intended to help you	15
CHAPTER 1: Turning compliance *'Push'* into employee *'Pull'*	21
CHAPTER 2: The Compliance & Ethics *'Passport'*	25
CHAPTER 3: *The Licensed Buyer, The Licensed Revenue Officer, Licensed Seller Licensed Marketeer* et al – Passport Derivatives	28
CHAPTER 4: Third-party and Team Compliance – *'Scores on the Doors'*	30
CHAPTER 5: The Compliance & Ethics *'Covenant'*	34
CHAPTER 6: Whistleblowing Hotlines & Helplines – *VeRoniCA*	39
CHAPTER 7: Whistleblowing Hotlines & Helplines – Testing & What Else?	48
CHAPTER 8: Retaliation – *The Reality*	52
CHAPTER 9: The EU Whistleblower Protection Directive's *'Reverse Burden of Proof'*	64
CHAPTER 10: World-class whistleblowing in eight *unconventional* steps	68
CHAPTER 11: *The Corporate Shield:* What's your Compliance & Ethics *Shield?*	83
CHAPTER 12: *How far would you go?*	88
CHAPTER 13: The Cost of Compliance & Other *Unconventional* Leadership Opportunities	94
CHAPTER 14: Compliance & Ethics *Nudge* – and *Sludge*	98
CHAPTER 15: *Positive* Conflicts of Interest	103
CHAPTER 16: *Engaging* Ethics	112

CHAPTER 17:	Compliance & Ethics Competitions and Group Activities: *The Opportunity*	116
CHAPTER 18:	Windscreens & Mirrors: *What gets measured gets managed*	124
CHAPTER 19:	Working with Works Councils in Europe	131
CHAPTER 20:	*Active* Anti-Bribery & Corruption: *Is It Reasonable, Could I Reciprocate?*	135
CHAPTER 21:	Compliance, Ethics – and *Practical* Persuasion	142
Appendix 1:	The Corporate Shield: *Assessing your Programmes*	148
Appendix 2:	The Corporate Shield: *Typical Compliance & Ethics Actions*	154
Appendix 3:	Anti-Retaliation Checklist *(including EU Whistleblower Protection Directive requirements)*	156
Appendix 4:	Working with Works Councils – Checklist	160
Appendix 5:	Implementing XYZ Co's new Hotline & Case Manager System *Works Councils: Typical Questions & Answers*	163
Appendix 6:	Conflicts of Interest (CoI): Programme Performance and Risk Assessment Questionnaire	171
Appendix 7:	*Compliance and Science* – The Telegraph	176

Notes, Links, References & Sources	181
Acknowledgements	185
About the Author	186
Index	187

For my grandchildren

Foreword

I came to my career in corporate ethics and compliance like many others, I suspect: I wandered into the field by chance, without understanding how rewarding it could be. Come to think of it, my friendship with Keith Read started much the same way.

By the time I met Keith in 2010, I had already been studying and writing about corporate compliance programs for several years. I had started as a contributing writer for Compliance Week in 2003, shortly after the Sarbanes-Oxley Act had been enacted in the United States — the first law that put true urgency behind corporate governance, audit, and compliance issues. In the ensuing years I rose to be editor of Compliance Week and the publication grew to be a voice for compliance professionals in the United States.

That said, we understood that corporate compliance was a global issue, and I needed more contacts from outside the United States. So I started searching online for compliance officers in London. Soon I found one Keith Read, then head of ethics and compliance for British Telecom (now simply BT).

Well, I thought, he must be someone who knows compliance in Britain. So I emailed him — and thus began one of the most enjoyable and rewarding professional relationships I've had in what is now 20 years of writing about corporate compliance. I have **never** had a conversation with Keith where he isn't brimming with enthusiasm, both for corporate compliance as a field and for compliance officers as people.

Keith grasps the central challenge of the modern corporate compliance officer: how to make corporate ethics and compliance **relevant** to employees, in a tangible and practical way.

After all, very few people outright oppose ethical conduct or obeying the law; they simply see corporate compliance programs as an esoteric thing without much practical utility to their "real" jobs. If they're employees on the workshop floor, they smile at your compliance presentation and then get on with their day as usual once you leave. If they're management, they talk about the importance of compliance publicly; and then behind the scenes, when trying to clean up an incident, ask the legal or compliance team, "How much do we need to pay to put this behind us?" because they see compliance programs as just a necessary cost for doing business.

Compliance officers need every tip, tool, and trick of the trade to scale those walls of disinterest. That's the advice, accumulated over many years as both an in-house compliance executive and an outside consultant, that Keith tries to impart in this book.

For example, the very first chapter in the book talks about how invert the relationship between compliance and the rest of the enterprise: away from the "push" dynamic of compliance officers nosing their way into a business function, toward a "pull" dynamic where business functions **want** to talk with the compliance team when encountering a problem or launching some new project. Every compliance officer would agree with the appeal of that idea — it's the desired state for compliance programs, really — but the painstaking work of persuasion and building alliances is the hard part. Keith offers his hard-fought wisdom on how to do that part.

We could go on from there, hop-scotching across all the other obstacles that compliance officers encounter: encouraging whistleblowers and discouraging retaliation; identifying the right metrics to monitor the progress of your compliance program; framing conversations about the compliance program the correct way (the "shield" metaphor is one that Keith uses) so that you can bring important issues to light with senior management.

Compliance officers reading this book could imagine it almost as a conversation with the author. It's written in a tone that's relaxed but not overly familiar, guided by the theory of best practices but also grounded in real-world experience (which — spoiler alert! — is not always what best practices tell us to expect). You can read it cover to cover for a comprehensive discussion; or read chapters as they catch your fancy, to help you think more sharply about the specific issue dogging you at that moment.

Perhaps I'm biased because of my friendship with Keith, but as I read through the book I couldn't help but hear his enthusiasm and expertise ring through. This is an author who doesn't just want to produce guidance that compliance professionals can consume; this is a person who wants fellow compliance officers to develop a deeper appreciation for what we all do — and then use that understanding as fuel to run a vibrant ethics and compliance program that your entire enterprise will value.

So put the book to good work, and enjoy.

Matt Kelly
Editor, Radical Compliance
Boston, USA

A personal introduction:
Compliance – *not Complacence*

My name is Keith Read. I was formerly the British Telecom (BT) Group Compliance and Ethics Director in the days that British Telecom (BT) was a very large £20 billion ($25 billion) privatised global company, with some 200,000 employees, tens of thousands of contractors, 6,300 buildings and operations in 176 countries; not surprisingly, managing the company's compliance and ethics represented quite a challenge.

Prior to first becoming the Group Regulatory Compliance Director, I was responsible for all governance and integrity across BT's £6 billion global supply chain. At that time, I had no idea that I would subsequently take responsibility for compliance, but it was a role that certainly stood me in good stead, and taught me much about ethical supply chains, and the challenges and opportunities of Environmental, Social and Governance (ESG).

As Compliance Director, I was fortunate enough to win a *Compliance Officer of the Year* award, which led to *The Daily Telegraph* publishing a full-page article – *Compliance and Science* – on how I had managed to turn around BT's compliance performance, something that had historically faced extensive scrutiny and criticism by regulators, government, the telecoms industry, competitors, customers and the press alike.

One incident during my tenure as BT's Compliance Director really brought home the reality of compliance and ethics, in this case related to a data protection issue. The murder of a man connected to a criminal gang resulted in his killer being arrested and going to prison. That should have been the end of the matter, but friends of the murdered man vowed they would pursue the killer's parents. The parents were offered witness protection but instead decided to leave their home and move elsewhere, in the hope that the threat would pass. However, some months later, after beginning their new life, they were tracked down to their new home and killed, using details from telephone records given to them by two corrupt (and, perhaps, naïve and frightened) BT employees. Reports about the consequences of compliance failure invariably bring up fines, reputational damage, resignations and dismissals of senior employees and, occasionally, prison sentences – but this example really does bring home the realities and the risks.

Since leaving BT, I have worked with and advised many international companies and organisations across a wide range of sectors including food, utilities, higher education and petrochemicals on their compliance, ethics, whistleblowing, data protection, culture, risk management, anti-fraud, anti-bribery and governance programmes, and have spoken in many parts of the world. I have also been an advisor for a number of years to LRN and to Convercent (now OneTrust). I have written extensively on compliance, ethics and related issues; a Google search will quickly turn up some examples.

So, that's me in a nutshell. But why have I written this book, and – most importantly – how is it intended to help you?

How this book is intended to help you

My job as BT's Regulatory Compliance Director at the outset was *simply* to turn around BT's compliance performance, an appointment largely triggered by increasingly vociferous and high-profile criticism from a raft of key stakeholders.

I was not the first Compliance Officer to be in that position – and I won't be the last – and it became immediately apparent that whatever I was going to do, it had to be different, innovative and compelling if it (and I) were going to be successful, and successful quickly.

I rapidly discovered that across many industries, sectors and companies, compliance is often perceived internally as the *Business Prevention Department*, *The Department of No* or one of a multitude of similar phrases that many readers will already be familiar with. That perception, albeit often unstated, is equally often largely held right across a company, and in places from *top-floor to shop floor*.

I also rapidly discovered that whilst most compliance officers, if not all, faced many similar and common challenges, I rarely attended a compliance-type event where there was an idea or approach that really stopped me in my tracks, gave me real pause for thought or represented a genuinely *unconventional* approach; there was lot of good, solid stuff that would support a good, solid compliance programme, but near-nothing that for me would make a radical difference and change the perception of many people who, arguably, saw compliance (and ethics) as some combination of bureaucratic, intrusive on their time and not an issue for them. They were – mostly – prepared to complete their compliance training when that came around and so tick the 'box' (more on that later) but, as an indication of their engagement, they often did the training quickly and perfunctorily, sometimes first thing in the morning or last thing in the evening to 'get it out of the way' and sometimes only after multiple reminders.

Whether readers perceive this as a negative or realistic view, it caused me to conclude that **doing things differently** was going to be central to our compliance and ethics programme. Getting to where we needed to be – with an effective programme that was respected and recognised by the same raft of key stakeholders – was going to need to be *unconventional* and innovative, and this book is simply intended to bring together some of the better compliance and ethics ideas, innovations, approaches and strategies that I have developed, encountered and utilised; innovations that go some way to address the perennial challenges that compliance and ethics officers face.

I would suggest that as a rough rule of thumb, 80% of compliance officers face broadly the same challenges; 20% might be specific to a particular company, industry, sector, geography or regulatory regime, but the majority will be largely common.

Ten typical examples of these perennial, common or core challenges for compliance officers would include:

  i. Understanding and addressing the range of potential compliance and ethics risks
  ii. Getting support from senior/top management
  iii. Managing internal and external relationships, including key stakeholders and regulatory-type bodies
  iv. Making best use of whatever resources are available
  v. Responding to change in compliance and ethics, including legislation, regulation, technology and societal (such as social media and social responsibility)

vi. Managing compliance and ethics internationally, including legislative developments and differences
vii. Implementing, establishing and operating effective training, education, communications, whistleblowing and disclosures (e.g. Conflicts of Interest and Gifts & Hospitality (G&H)/Gifts, Travel & Entertainment (GT&E))
viii. Getting employees and contractors (and anyone in a work-based relationship with a company) engaged and committed, and indifference addressed
ix. Managing compliance and ethics in what can be a four- or five-generation workplace
x. Addressing the challenge of third-parties and third-party risk, utilising process, systems and genuine engagement

Clearly, the approaches in this book may not be appropriate to every organisation; what I do hope, though, is that most will be directly relevant to your company and the challenges that you face, and that others will help your thinking on your own compliance and ethics journey.

This book is not intended as an introduction to compliance – a *Compliance 101* – but it does give unconventional, new and novel ideas, approaches and strategies right across the compliance officer's spectrum, including some intended to address or mitigate what are, arguably, the most intransigent and universal issues. Arguably, it will not take long for these issues to arise for you – whether you are new to compliance and ethics, in a new role or in a new company – and so I would like to hope there is relatively little doubt that the book will be appropriate as you, and your role, develop.

Although I have previously written about elements of these strategies, this is the first time that they have been brought together in one place in this way. I have kept the book purposely short so that it should be relatively quick and easy to read, such that readers do not have to wade through lengthy text and 'legalese' to get to ideas and concepts that could change their compliance and ethics programmes and, hopefully, their reputations and careers – and serve to turn *The Department of No* into the widely-respected *Department of Know*.

If you were to ask colleagues and others about the likely consequences of compliance issues and failures, they will invariably bring up issues around fines, reputational damage, resignations and dismissals of senior employees and, occasionally, prison sentences; after all, that's what is mostly in the press.

However, there can be other unexpected – and appalling – consequences of compliance failure, and this book highlights my experiences of some of those, such as the arguably naïve, perhaps frightened but nevertheless corrupt employees whose actions resulted in a double murder, and the whistleblower retaliation that resulted in attempted suicide by the employee's child. Extreme examples you may say, but my experience is that such examples can often serve to bring home and embed the message far more effectively and powerfully than hours of training, and it is for this reason that they have been included.

I often talk to compliance and ethics officer colleagues about being *Big & Bold* with their compliance programme, and innovative. As part of that, I also ask what their top *three wins* of compliance would be; that is, what would *good* look like for their compliance and ethics programme, and what would be the three key indicators? These are my *three wins* of compliance: A *demonstrably compliant organisation* – recognised and respected as such, operating at a *minimum or optimal Cost of Compliance* with a *recognised compliance capability and reputation* – expertise that can be leveraged or marketed.

Clearly, the third may not be appropriate to all companies; in my case, however, not only did that recognised compliance capability facilitate a step change in the relationship with the regulator, it also laid the foundations for a successful business unit that provided compliance support solutions to other organisations.

However, some of the key challenges for me related to determining what regulations and legislation we had to comply with – both in letter and spirit, how well were we complying and how I could prove it if the day came that I needed to. This resulted for me in the concept of **Demonstrable Compliance**, such that I could be compliant and be able to demonstrate it; it would clearly be unacceptable to say that the company was compliant, yet be unable to demonstrate it confidently, continuously and effectively. In this vein, regulators on both sides of the Atlantic will often want extensive information (and data) on the metrics that are utilised in a compliance programme, a key aspect that we consider later.

Each chapter is largely standalone, although some core issues – such as retaliation – are considered from different angles in different chapters. However, each chapter in this book contains *unconventional* ways – such as the **Corporate Shield** – and tips and insights into *doing things differently* to address, or influence, what are the perennial challenges of compliance and ethics. I do hope that readers will give me feedback on their own ideas, and also how the approaches featured here worked for them. I know that some have been directly, and successfully, adopted by compliance officers in major companies that I have worked with, and I hope that they are equally successful for you.

Keith Read
Hampshire, UK
2022

Chapter 1: Turning compliance *'Push'* into employee *'Pull'*

I would suggest that most, if not all, compliance and ethics officers around the world, regardless of industry, sector, geography or regulatory regime, spend their time *pushing* – such that *push* is central to compliance and ethics programmes in the vast majority of companies globally; *pushing* out the training, *pushing* out the training reminders, *pushing* out the escalations, *pushing* out the communications emails and so on.

Not surprisingly, this leads to compliance *fatigue* and *push back* from employees and others on the *receiving* end, and consequently a host of potential issues for the compliance function. Clearly, some sectors – particularly financial and also legal services – have a compliance qualification regime that drives engagement of many employees, as without their qualifications, they are unable to practise – but not every sector benefits from this type of incentivisation.

Put simply, *push* is a staple for the vast majority of global compliance and ethics programmes and, indeed, 'campaigns'-type platforms now offer the facility to automate much of this process – whether it is in relation to training completions, Conflict of Interest declarations, policy acknowledgements or a host of other compliance-related activities.

However, whilst these platforms are increasingly sophisticated and offer messaging, targeting, follow-up, exception/excuse management and bespoke analytics, they arguably only serve to promulgate some of the real and key challenges for compliance officers such as employee fatigue, indifference, *ticking the box*, *genuine* engagement and commitment; the challenge can be even greater where it involves contractors or third parties (which we will consider separately later).

Many companies take a largely similar approach to their compliance training and education regime; in broad terms, it generally involves the creation of a compliance email communications campaign for a particular piece of training and then subsequent follow-up with employees, contractors and others that are 'in scope' again by email if they fail to complete the training by the required date; coupled also perhaps with text reminders, email follow-up is often undertaken twice which, however unacceptable, is simply pragmatic.

After that, follow-up could involve a personal phone call and, potentially, escalation to the individual's manager and beyond. Clearly, this is both time-consuming and expensive – and by the time someone has received multiple reminders, in reality they are treating the training as a 'chore' and so the learning and benefit for everyone is diminished – but most compliance officers have a razor focus on the 'input' measure, which is purely training completions, so they stick with it; after all, those measures are often central to their board reporting, and to their personal remuneration/reward. Given this, we will cover the challenges – and key opportunities – around compliance 'input' and 'output' measure examples later. Moreover, employees, contractors and others in a *work-based relationship* who do not have company email access can represent a further challenge and risk, and **reaching the wider workforce** is an opportunity that we will also consider later.

In common with most compliance officers, I grew tired fairly quickly of the push back, indifference and excuses that we encountered in doing the follow-up – push back which was pretty serious at times and, on occasion, can come from senior employees, some of whom it appeared were involved in having secretaries, assistants and colleagues complete training on behalf of others. Arguably, some of this can have its roots in history, with compliance training being often perceived as an inconsequential and time-consuming 'box-ticking' exercise – but it is unacceptable behaviour, and cannot continue if compliance officers are going to genuinely deliver *demonstrable compliance*; a compliant company with the ability to readily demonstrate that compliance.

However, these issues served to start me thinking about how I could **turn compliance *push* into employee *pull*** – where employees (and others) genuinely wanted to receive compliance and ethics-related materials because they were interesting and interested – and they recognised their importance and the real risks that they were addressing. It also made me think about my college studies when I was in my teens; I still remember many of those lessons now because they were important to me, and I wanted to learn. The challenge was *simply* to achieve the same now with compliance and ethics.

In common with many other compliance and ethics officers, I'd had several discussions with my HR colleagues and others about including compliance and ethics in annual employee performance reviews. However, these discussions never got that far because of a number of not unreasonable concerns – including whether compliance and ethics was too specific to warrant an individual performance marking and, perhaps, the potential risk of rewarding what was potentially perceived as *over-compliance*.

To me, changing compliance *push* to employee *pull* was crucial to fundamentally changing compliance and ethics such that we had a self-sustaining programme that drove change, minimised unnecessary chasing and *persuasion* resources and was genuinely successful.

A great idea, you may say – but how can you deliver it in practice? Over the coming chapters, I have outlined some of the key *push* to *pull* approaches that I came up with which, I would suggest, are certainly worth considering for your programme. Clearly, competitions, games and associated reward processes also have a role in the ***pull equation***, some innovative aspects of which we will also consider later.

Core to this success, however, it is essential to consider the people and teams involved and affected, whilst never losing sight of the ***what's in it for me?*** question seen from their viewpoint, and how that question can be addressed. Otherwise, some people may think that compliance is being *done to them* and so avoid, delay or defer training, declarations, attestations or acknowledgements – and the benefit to the company and individual alike will be lost or, at best, diminished.

Thinking through the *what's in it for me?* question is something, I would suggest, that is not always fully considered, nor is how the 'levers' – the wider tools and techniques – potentially available to a compliance officer can be fully utilised. For example, if compliance training can be used to increase an individual's educational and professional qualifications which are, in turn, a key parameter in gaining advancement or promotion, then compliance training may well be perceived in a different light.

A number of readers will be familiar with the concepts enshrined in the *Technology Acceptance Model (TAM)*, which is a systems theory that models how people come to accept and use technology. In particular, it not unexpectedly suggests that both ease-of-use and usefulness of the technology affect *behavioural intention*, and hence user experience and acceptance. Turning compliance *push* into employee *pull* is one element of what I termed the comparable **Compliance & Ethics Acceptance Model** (**CEAM**); this is an invaluable consideration in compliance and ethics programme implementation, including the qualities that would make the programme engaging, accepted, utilised and recognised such that there was resulting behavioural change. Crucially, it also considered the degree of *hysteresis* in the programme, i.e. the longer-term sustainability, persistence and maintenance of compliance and ethics performance after the initial roll-out profile and energy has diminished.

Chapter 2: Compliance & Ethics *'Passport'*

Most companies and organisations have some form of compliance training regime, usually with a degree of differentiation based on an individual's seniority, role or responsibilities. The Learning Management System (LMS), Training Records System (TRS) or related system usually records these completions and that is usually the end of the matter, until the next refresh completion in one to five years' time, unless additional training is injected in the meantime for some legislative, specialist risk or other reason.

Whilst failing to complete the training will usually generate multiple reminders, escalations and other consequences, completing the training on time often generates very little, other than – perhaps – the opportunity to generate a simple certificate which will rarely, if ever, be referred to.

The ***Compliance and Ethics Passport***, however, changes all this; it means that once an individual's training and other related actions are up to date, they have their passport, a more formal, valuable and durable certification of their achievement.

It also offers the opportunity to make it a more celebrated and recognised achievement, and the passport becomes a prerequisite for an employee to be able to apply for jobs, promotions and other opportunities; moreover, it serves to send a powerful message of leadership and *doing the right thing* to regulators and similar bodies.

The passport could also potentially form the basis of a recognised qualification at company level and, in my experience, the *passport opportunity* can be greatly welcomed and respected by employees – some of whom may not have many, or even any, existing qualifications.

Clearly, the concept behind the Compliance and Ethics Passport was simply that it gave a more tangible – and potentially useable – recognition of the training that an individual had undertaken in compliance; as a consequence, the compliance training has demonstrable value to the individual, whilst supporting the company in being compliant, and achieving *demonstrable compliance*.

Crucially, in broad terms, a major European company might expect an annual employee turnover ('churn') of around 4% – but against that, individual contractor turnover is likely to be nearer 30% and it is here that the passport also has a potentially key role in maintaining a compliance regime, whilst minimising the cost of that regime.

Clearly, to be even more effective and useful, the qualification would ideally need to be collaborative and portable – recognised by other companies and by relevant regulators, which would then also serve to move an industry a little way towards the financial services qualification-type regime.

Irrespective of the appetite in a wider industry sector for such a qualification, the principle clearly conveys the message – to government, regulators and others – that there is a demonstrable commitment to compliance in a company, or companies within that industry, and evidences their lead role in *better compliance*. This could also represent a useful stance in response to government-led initiatives around *better regulation*.

As we will see later, the compliance passport is just one potential element of the Compliance Covenant, an approach which goes some way to address the *what's in it for me?* element of compliance.

Under the Covenant, an additional approach could be to 'gate' or restrict an individual's annual performance review marking, dependent upon achievement of their compliance passport or, more simply, completion of their compliance training.

The same approach can be used regarding reward for performance against objectives, so that although compliance may not be an explicit objective, it is nonetheless implicit.

Clearly, the use of positive incentives and – crucially – the avoidance of disincentives both have a key role to play in compliance attainment, and in the Compliance and Ethics *Covenant*, as we will consider shortly.

An incentive, for example, would be that the Compliance and Ethics Passport is seen and used as a qualification, thus recognising and rewarding individuals who complete the process. Avoiding disincentives (e.g. allowing the passport to fall into abeyance, not differentiating sufficiently between passport holders and others) is also equally important.

Some of the 'softer' passport-related incentives could include, for example, entering passport holders into a regular prize drawing, although it is not considered that this type of approach should generally be used as a significant compliance management tool.

However, from personal experience, a prize competition for early completers of compliance training did generate extensive interest – which whilst perhaps slightly surprising, did facilitate dialogue and a number of new opportunities.

Chapter 3: *The Licensed Buyer, The Licensed Revenue Officer, Licensed Seller, Licensed Marketeer* et al – **Passport Derivatives**

What are the roles and role groups within your company that represent the greatest compliance and ethics risk? For example, call centre operations may represent particular risk for your company given the nature of the business and the degree of regulation. However, almost without exception, procurement, revenue (sales) and marketing will come at, or near, the top of any company compliance and ethics risk chart largely because of ever-present risks around regulation, competition/anti-trust, ethics, bribery and corruption, as examples.

Many companies clearly provide general compliance and ethics training, but some also implement bespoke, role-specific training to address these types of risk. Given this background, the Compliance and Ethics Passport does not have to be a specially created and standalone qualification and, indeed, it can be incorporated into other company qualifications, both existing and new.

For example, a procurement role brings with it a range of crucial process requirements – which include compliance and ethics – that must be discharged properly if a company is not to find itself facing a raft of issues, including appeals and disgruntled unsuccessful tenderers, potentially in the courts.

For this reason, companies increasingly establish their own internal training, qualification and accreditation regimes and, clearly, such tailored programmes – for example, a *Licensed Buyer Scheme* – offer a crucial vehicle to incorporate role-specific compliance and ethics training and testing into a high-risk group.

It also introduces what is both a control and incentive that employees are not allowed to purchase on behalf of the company unless they are licensed which, from personal experience, can also have the additional – and recognisable – benefit of bringing greater control to who is buying and, hence, spending monies on behalf of the company.

Put simply, the Licensed Buyer Scheme can be developed to incorporate the Compliance and Ethics Passport, providing an important composite qualification regime for supply chain employees.

Moreover, there is no reason why parallel bespoke schemes – covering revenue (sales), marketing and other activities where there is significant compliance and ethics risk – could not be similarly established to develop professional standing and performance, whilst also incorporating key aspects of compliance and ethics.

Chapter 4: Third-party & Team Compliance – *'Scores on the Doors'*

Third-party compliance has relatively quickly grown into a significant issue for many, if not most, companies and their compliance officers. This growth has been driven by a range of factors, not least of all increased outsourcing, greater regulatory scrutiny and recognition that responsibility for compliance and ethics does not stop at the office door or factory gate, and that third parties can represent significant risks to the companies that contract with them; typical risks include contractual performance, reputation, cyber, data privacy, corruption, modern slavery and governance. Moreover, related international legislation – such as the EU Whistleblower Protection Directive – is multiplying, and increasingly recognising the role and associated risks of third parties, as we will see.

Third-Party Risk Management (TPRM) focuses on identifying and reducing the risks related to the use of third parties which can include (but is not limited to) vendors, suppliers, partners, contractors and service providers. Put simply, whilst a company can outsource an activity, it cannot just outsource the associated compliance and ethics risks.

As a consequence of the increased recognition of risk in this area, it would take moments to find a raft of technology platforms designed to help mitigate third-party risk. At its heart, TPRM (and the associated Due Diligence) is the process of identifying, measuring and managing the compliance, ethics and other risks that a third party poses to a company. TPRM evaluates and helps management of those risks by evaluating companies and the business relationship based on a list of weighted criteria related to security, privacy, IT, capability and others leading to automated risk tiering, and also ongoing monitoring.

Based on that evaluation and when it is undertaken in the procurement and supply process, the vendor/supplier would typically be given the opportunity to resolve issues and reduce its risk to the evaluating company. However, a high-risk vendor may be discounted in the procurement process, or deemed to require additional monitoring and follow-up; in worst cases, any relationship may be severed. Clearly, that is not the end of the process for critical vendors, as TPRM can then be deployed – depending on its sophistication – to monitor for adverse media and crucial compliance and ethics events over time.

Clearly, the objective of TPRM is to reduce risk and ensure that third parties align with a company's values, ethos, ethics and similar characteristics. However, there are increasingly high-profile concerns that regardless of how increasingly sophisticated TPRM platforms become, consistently achieving genuinely compliant and ethical third parties is a different matter.

Put simply, whilst the technology may be great, a regularly-reported plaintive cry is 'Why won't they comply?' – and it's here that third parties face the 'usual' compliance challenges, not least of all because genuine compliance requires genuine willingness, commitment and determination on behalf of the third party within the right processes and *enabling environment*.

So, whilst a sophisticated TPRM platform will provide data-driven automation of the end-to-end, third-party management processes, the challenge – and opportunity – is clearly to achieve a risk-based third-party compliance regime in which there is high confidence, and where third parties are genuinely engaged. Building that bridge between platform and practice is the issue, and this was my approach.

The vast majority of restaurants, cafés, pubs, clubs and takeaways in the UK display their hygiene rating, based on a one-to-five-star system measured by their local authority; it has now become formally known as the **Scores on the Doors** scheme. Many other countries and their states have adopted similar schemes.

In a light-bulb moment, what came from that approach for me was that, although a company may require individual employees to complete compliance training and then undergo some form of testing of their knowledge, there was no single and straightforward indicator of a third-party, supplier, vendor or team's compliance capability or performance; a team in this context could be 10, 100, 1,000 or 10,000 people.

As a consequence, as part of the Compliance and Ethics Covenant, the concept of a team compliance rating system was established, driven by a number of parameters – including compliance training completion levels, failure rates, numbers of *serial offenders* (i.e. employees and contractors who had consistently failed to complete their training on time) and senior management compliance training performance, which included levels of attendance at special briefing and educational sessions.

This 'hygiene rating' system has the benefit that it also establishes a degree of compliance-related competition between teams, units and divisions, and facilitates an additional board-level reporting measure, achievement awards and similar supporting recognition.

One acid test for any company's compliance and ethics strategy is whether that strategy does, indeed, touch every part, layer and function in the organisation; this is depicted in the inverted triangle approach shown in Figure 1, and 'Scores on the Doors' provides a way of demonstrably measuring the performance of teams, factories, call centres, divisions, geographies, senior teams, the board and, indeed, the company as a whole.

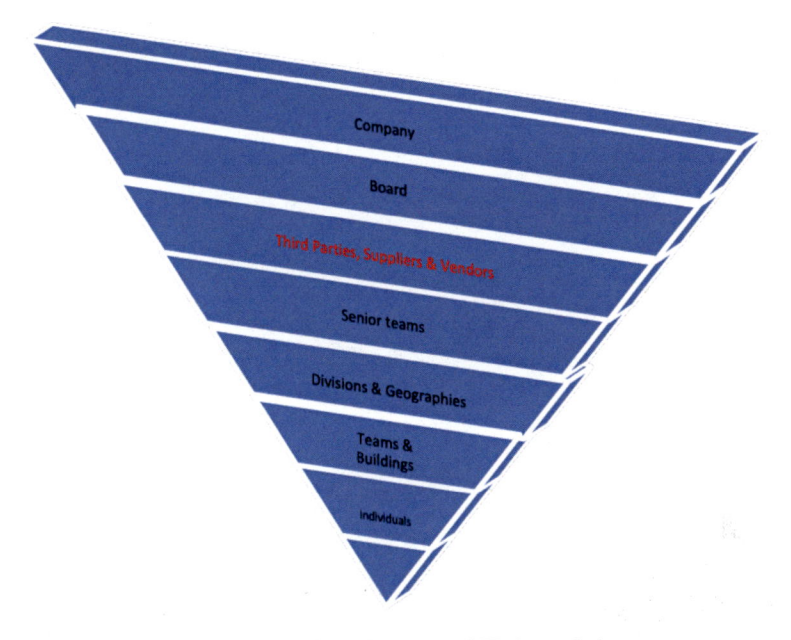

Figure 1: 'The Inverted Triangle'

By extending *Scores on the Doors* and 'hygiene ratings' to third parties, suppliers and vendors, this can become a very powerful governance motivator for what are critical collaborators, who can be external and remote but, depending on their role, can also be embedded within their client company – to the point that it is difficult to immediately differentiate between employees and third-party contractors.

Do not underestimate the value and importance of a five-star *Scores on the Doors* compliance and ethics award to a third party, vendor or supplier – and the potential benefit and recognition they will accrue from being invited (for example) to the annual five-star award-winners' dinner and presentation. Moreover, those that aspire to achieving five-star status will be more engaged and determined across the spectrum of compliance and ethics, and so the low-cost *Scores on the Doors* programme becomes a high-value tool in the compliance and ethics officer's armoury.

Chapter 5: The Compliance & Ethics *'Covenant'*

I have frequently heard an argument, made by a range of attendees at compliance and ethics events and meetings, that without the qualification-type infrastructure of the financial services industry, compliance officers have relatively few tools at their disposal to genuinely drive up the focus on, and engagement with, compliance.

Put simply, the Compliance Covenant goes some way to address the *what's in it for me?* element of the **compliance equation**; the compliance passport, Scores on the Doors and other techniques seen earlier are key supporting elements to the Compliance Covenant.

The dictionary definition of a covenant is that it is an agreement, usually formal, between two or more persons to do, or not do, something specified. A variation of that definition is that it is a formal agreement between two or more people; a promise.

The Military or Armed Forces Covenant (www.armedforcescovenant.gov.uk) is a term used in the UK which reflects the duty of care that the country has to those who serve, or have served, in its armed forces. In return for putting the needs of the armed forces and the nation before their own, British services people and their families must always be able to expect fair treatment, and to be valued and respected as individuals. A similar Police Covenant has also now been published.

As already outlined, I had become increasingly concerned that many employees (and others) perceived compliance and ethics as the *Business*

Prevention Department, with the consequence that anything compliance-related was seen as a 'chore' by many, without any real understanding of the risks – specific and generic – that were being addressed. Many, I believed, considered that compliance was an unnecessary distraction with little or no relevance to their role and so was being *done to them*.

However, from that, it occurred to me that a Compliance and Ethics *Covenant* – something that enshrined many of the elements and principles of the Armed Forces Covenant could serve to reset, re-establish and maintain the compliance relationship, and provide the basis for a compliance and ethics agreement, with attestation if required. The Covenant would make clear that compliance was central to the operation of the company and, as a consequence, was an essential commitment by everyone regardless of their role.

One of the most common – and most discussed – challenges for compliance and ethics officers is that of ensuring that everyone in a company, from the board down, 'signs up' to compliance, such that they understand the need for compliance, what compliance and ethics mean for them, and why they need to – willingly – undertake training and other compliance obligations relevant to them. *Tone at the Top, Tone in the Middle* and a host of related compliance and ethics terms all relate to securing and maintaining this commitment.

I'm sure that many compliance and ethics officers reading this – whatever their background, industry or geography – will recognise that challenge but, in case you're not convinced, just take a look at the number of compliance events that feature sessions along the lines of *changing compliance behaviours, improving compliance programme effectiveness, changing the compliance culture* or *making the case for compliance*.

I accept that some industries, such as financial services, have a compliance training and certification regime intended to debar individuals if they are not qualified. However, most industries, companies and organisations do not, and this is where the Compliance and Ethics Covenant comes in. Phrasing in the Covenant such as *I would never ask you to do anything that I would not do, but anything that I ask you to do, you have to do* from the Chief Executive Officer (CEO), Chief Ethics and Compliance Officer (CECO) or General Counsel can be very powerful, and very persuasive – and reinforces the message that effective compliance depends on everyone.

Training is inevitably at the heart of an effective compliance and ethics programme, but often, despite their best endeavours, compliance officers struggle to deliver acceptable completion rates, largely because the training invariably takes second place to the latest business pressure, and there is neither genuine and active support nor effective mandate from senior management. Moreover, even if the completion rates are acceptable, the level of actual learning can be a long way from ideal.

Whilst compliance training of itself would, clearly, not make a company compliant, it is nevertheless a key generic element in the 'Corporate Shield'. Low completion levels make it near-impossible to argue with regulators, the courts, critics, commentators and competitors that there is a company-wide ethos of compliance and ethical performance.

By accident or design, companies and organisations can often pay 'lip service' to compliance, which only serves to make the compliance officer's job more difficult. Compliance horror stories abound – of assistants undertaking their manager's compliance training and, worse, with individuals completing the training for entire offices or teams. Perhaps some readers won't believe this, or have never encountered it, but it happens.

To compound matters, this behaviour can be effectively condoned by some senior managers who have their secretaries complete their training and then turn a blind eye to everyone else. Not only are people being passive in not doing what is required of them, arguably the only time that they are active is when it comes to avoiding completing their training!

To be fair, whilst I may have perhaps exaggerated the scenarios above, I am sure that some of the situations will strike a chord with many compliance and ethics officers.

The Compliance and Ethics Covenant, however, offers a way of fundamentally changing this situation through a pragmatic scheme – effectively, an agreement – that generates wider benefit from compliance, both for the company and for employees as individuals, without 'over-compliance'. It also serves to raise the profile of compliance in the company and to get the compliance message firmly embedded in people's minds.

I fully accept that employees should recognise the importance of compliance – and most do, when pressed. However, the Compliance and Ethics Covenant would not diminish that in any way, nor would it remove the potential for compliance-related disciplinary sanctions.

What it does do, however, is serve to raise the perception of compliance and ethics such that they become more of a business and personal essential – rather than a chore – that effectively turns conscripts into volunteers.

The Compliance and Ethics Covenant is a simple, personal agreement that says, for example, that the company will not ask an employee to undertake any training or similar compliance activity that is not essential, appropriate and relevant to that person as an individual and employee. However, in return, anything that the company does ask an employee (or contractor) to do is important and, as a consequence, it should be completed diligently and to the required schedule.

My experience – using a passionately written Compliance Covenant delivered to everyone in the company from the most senior to the most junior – was that it fundamentally shifted the perception of compliance;

largely, this was because for the first time it was more personalised – and certainly pulled no punches about why compliance is important.

What are now known as 'nudge' techniques also played a key part in the effectiveness of this and subsequent communications, an aspect that we will consider later in this book.

Clearly, offering incentives to employees to fulfil compliance training requirements, and giving recognition to those who successfully complete the programme, perhaps in a particular timescale, is one way to engage workers in a compliance culture. Whilst I experimented with all manner of incentives for employees to complete their training – including individual and team prize draws, rewards and recognition – I was never satisfied that these incentives were anything other than short-term; the Compliance and Ethics Covenant and the associated elements, however, serve to bring together both incentive and longer-term culture change.

Chapter 6: Whistleblowing, Hotlines & Helplines – *VeRoniCA*

Invariably, one of the perennial challenges for compliance and ethics officers is around whistleblowing, and hotlines and helplines.

A number of companies that I have worked with start out with a hotline that is internal, with reports typically routed to the security, legal, HR or compliance teams. I am certainly not saying that internal hotlines are bad, and external hotlines are good, however handling a security report is one thing but – even with specialist training – dealing with a potentially very nervous and distressed whistleblower with a complex report is another.

One question I would ask is whether you have ever **tested your own company's hotline**? In my experience, relatively few companies take this approach, and certainly not regularly. In one company's case, I became so concerned about their internal hotline that I made seven test reports, including one in school-level French, that were all compliance-type issues such that I knew where and to whom they should be routed. The outcome was that we only received two of the seven reports, and the handling of the report involving French translation was so appalling and time-consuming that it would have deterred even the most determined reporter.

Upon investigation, one of the many issues that emerged was that hotline reports were not the primary role of the security team to whom reports were being routed, such that their priorities were elsewhere. As a result, they were essentially performing their own informal triage on reports, because they (and their immediate managers) believed that minimising reports (and distractions from their primary role) was the right thing to do. The 'box had been ticked' that the company had a hotline, but the security team – mostly used to receiving reports of theft, fraud and suchlike – were dealing with hotline reports on a 'transactional' basis and many would-be reporters were lost because they became nervous when faced with the investigative style of questioning of a security team largely staffed by former police officers. Crucially, this meant that not only was the company losing a significant number of reports, but also reports from higher-risk locations were very limited – with the consequence that its ability to build a wider compliance risk picture was being compromised. In this company's case, this was the last straw, and the test was the catalyst for the company to move to an external hotline provider.

Having implemented a hotline – internal or external – the issue for the vast majority of compliance officers then becomes how do you get people – employees and others – to use it? It's here that I would suggest that a compliance and ethics officer has to be *unconventional*, and prepared to consider a range of tools and techniques in relation to their hotline.

A common experience of compliance and ethics officers is that employees (and contractors) perceive making a report to the hotline to be a (very) major step; something not to be undertaken lightly and something that perhaps goes against their very upbringing where, right from school, they learn never to *tell the teacher*. This perception can be reinforced by managers who will sometimes tell their team – directly or indirectly – that *we deal with any issues ourselves* and so they should not make a hotline report. You may question that statement, but you will be surprised by its prevalence; after all, managers will often have a vested interest in minimising the level of hotline reports relevant to them as – arguably – an adverse hotline report will rarely bring good news, and might well involve them in additional work; worst case, it might also affect their annual review, result in questions about their abilities and affect their pay and promotion prospects.

There are a range of factors that can result in potential reporters being deterred from making a hotline report, whether that is via phone, online/

web, open-door (manager/'proxy') and other channels. Crucially, it is easy to assume that a report made to a hotline is a 'transaction' and treat it as such; *this happened, they did this and these were the consequences*. However, from personal experience of a very large number of verbal reports, reporters can be very distressed, barely able to talk and in tears. They may also have delayed their report for months, perhaps whilst they talked it through with friends and family or, sometimes, waiting for individuals, managers and others involved to move on. It is for this reason that, increasingly, some – but certainly not all – hotline providers are starting to provide an **escrow**-type facility, such that a reporter can make a contemporaneous report whilst the incident is fresh in their mind without it being immediately forwarded to their company or organisation. This approach brings other options and benefits and is outlined more fully later.

As we have seen, the decision to report is often not taken lightly, a situation influenced by a range of factors; clearly, culture and upbringing play a part, but also uncertainty about where the report will go, who will know and what will happen to the individual as the reporter are also key factors. Again, from personal experience, these issues can be exacerbated in locations and countries where a company has a small presence; an employee may be in a small office sitting directly opposite the very manager about whom they wish to make a hotline report. However, they have no idea – and perhaps little confidence – whether their report will get back to that manager, directly or indirectly, and whether their report will remain truly confidential or anonymous given the relative ease by which they could be identified from within a small group by a simple process of elimination.

These *barriers to reporting* – barriers that prevent employees from reporting – can present a significant challenge to a company, and to the compliance function; again, whilst employees may not be familiar at all with the hotline, how it is operated and what 'confidential' and 'anonymous' mean in reality, perceptions can be all, however ill-informed and inaccurate those might be. Undertaking a robust and determined review and surveys of your own company's actual and perceived barriers to reporting can be a powerful tool to help improve whistleblowing specifically, and compliance performance in general. Crucially, however, at the centre of these barriers is inevitably the question of trust, which manifests itself in a number of ways that have already been outlined; I would suggest that questions such as *who will know?* and *who will find out?* are rarely far from a potential whistleblower's mind. However, build trust in all the facets of your hotline, address those types of question directly and its reputation will grow, and the reports will start to come.

Analytics are invariably crucial to an effective whistleblowing process, and they can be very revealing; for example, locations, functions and employee groups making few, or no, hotline reports or hotline reports confined to generic rather than specific issues. In my case, such data only served to increase my concerns over the perceived size of the 'step' in people's minds to making a report. As a consequence, we took the decision to provide both a hotline and a **helpline** as essentially integrated reporting channels, with the intention of removing, or at least minimising the 'step', and the concerns employees might have about reporting to the hotline.

However, I also had concerns that terms and taglines such as *hotline, speak-up line, integrity line* and others might not necessarily convey key messages such that we were open, welcoming and receptive, and without those the perceived 'step' might well remain. Crucially, I wanted to achieve a more approachable hotline, in the belief that that might open up reporting from a swathe of people who would never normally make contact.

Given these issues, I decided to go one stage further; we decided to brand the hotline and thus created **VeRoniCA** – **our Virtual Regulatory Compliance Assistant** – who is shown in Figure 2; branding, or naming, compliance in this way served to give compliance 'a face' – which, in turn, provided greater reassurance and support to employees, together with the perception of easier access.

It also represented a genuine attempt to combine hotline and helpline functionality – as opposed to simply re-badging a hotline as a 'helpline' – and whilst some reports and were definitely hotline and others definitely helpline, there was a surprising level of migration particularly between helpline and hotline, where initial questions turned into something more concerning and serious. Some other companies with whom I have discussed this technique have adopted a similar approach, and their feedback has been equally positive.

Figure 2: *VeRoniCA*: **Courtesy of British Telecom (BT)**

Put simply, this approach was intended to get people used to contacting *VeRoniCA* – and *Ask VeRoniCA* came into common parlance within the company, and people were perceived as now more prepared and used to raising issues. *VeroniCA* served to provide a channel to raise issues semi-formally whilst also facilitating escalation direct to the hotline if deemed appropriate; in this way, the major step often associated with calling the hotline itself was mitigated.

Moreover, *VeRoniCA* facilitated direct, indirect and *subliminal* messaging including direct messaging via email and indirect messaging via posters etc.; life-sized cardboard cut-outs of *VeRoniCA* were also used in building receptions and other areas to reinforce the compliance and ethics message very effectively.

I would suggest that communicating awareness of your hotline, and hotline reporting, hinges crucially on *leaving no stone unturned* and being prepared to experiment.

For example, **posters in washrooms (toilets)** have historically often been the stalwart of hotline communications, but putting those posters on the inside of stall/cubicle doors can be important, not least of all because it will not expose the employee's possible interest in the hotline to anyone else.

Put **posters** around the offices, sites, plants, etc. Use tear-off strips on posters (the sort of thing used for second-hand sales etc.) so that people can take hotline contact details with them, not forgetting to tear-off a couple of strips at the outset so that people perceive that they are not alone, and their colleagues are also using the hotline.

If 40% (say) of your employee base are drivers, then putting hotline details on company car and vehicle windscreen/windshield stickers, discs or licence holders can clearly pay dividends.

What about **payslips**? Regardless of how it is delivered, a good proportion of employees won't read their payslip if their pay is relatively consistent month-to-month, but an equally good proportion will, particularly where they have overtime, bonus, incentive and similar additions which vary – and that may well be the very employee population group where hotline reporting has been traditionally low. This is one potential example of a useful technique for ***reaching the wider workforce***.

What about employee **identity or passcards**? The front might be used for photographic and other details of the holder, but could the rear be used for compliance and the hotline? Given their role, these cards are often used by employees (and others) daily, such that it's an opportunity not to be missed.

Employee restaurant/canteen/dining room menus and other information are often placed on tables, where large numbers of employees (and others) dine every day. Why not use those for the hotline, or put a hotline-specific version on the table if nothing else suitable exists. In this case, just a subliminal consultation or awareness can be both invaluable, and crucial.

Codes of Conduct are often extensive documents of 50 pages or more and, as a consequence, can be deemed as intimidating, complicated and irrelevant. However, turn those 50 pages into a Z-Card folding version – with the hotline details featured on the outside cover – and suddenly a Code of Conduct becomes more accessible, relevant and easy-to-access, as do the hotline details. Crucially, it is ideal for a wallet or purse, and is more likely to be ready-to-hand if, and when, needed.

Extending that approach further, if historically a **hard-to-reach employee group** has been field engineers, then focus on what would make the difference; a good example is if they need to wipe their safety spectacles regularly then provide them with a spectacle cloth featuring the hotline and other compliance information that they might not normally, readily and regularly refer to.

The above are just a few examples of how to increase awareness of the hotline, through things that employees use regularly and may well already exist.

But what else can a compliance officer do to drive hotline reporting levels? Clearly, it's essential to make as many types of reporting channel available as possible, and recognise (and address) the challenges of your particular audience.

Offering a wider range of reporting methods can often be achieved at low cost, or with low barriers to entry. Whilst, for example, text/SMS has much to recommend it, lower-tech reporting via open-door (manager/'proxy'), email, postal mail and posting boxes can serve to offer alternatives, and meet the needs of particular situations and employee groups. However, it's also crucial to consider potential pitfalls – such as the well-intentioned company that, understandably, thought they were doing the right thing by putting hotline posting boxes in high-footfall areas in their offices, factories and sites without thinking that reporters might avoid them because of the likelihood of being seen and exposed. There are also confidentiality and security issues to be considered, but those have to be considered as part of the **whistleblowing equation** and balanced against the potentially wider reporter base.

It is important to give real thought to two further aspects of your company's hotline. Firstly, it can be intimidating for an employee to access your company's hotline page; is my access monitored, who will know, will I be seen, what will *they* do and suchlike. So, the opportunity is to use arguably *unconventional* ways of counteracting these issues; one example is to really consider and list likely issues such as this, and address them directly.

A further example is that there is extensive academic research around the *science of cuteness*, and how it can elicit positive emotions in unexpected contexts. Cute animal, cat, dog and similar images, for example, can result in activation of the pleasure centre of the brain, and in the release of dopamine – which is the same chemical that is released in powerfully positive circumstances, such as when people fall in love; it's for this reason that dogs are frequently used in photos on dating sites to make people appear more attractive. Crucially, cuteness is a way to stimulate and achieve *positive emotions in unexpected contexts* and so including such images on your hotline page can pay significant dividends by both helping to reduce intimidation and also setting a positive environment, as we will see later. As an extension of this, changing the images periodically can result in return visits and, hence, familiarity and reduced anxiety when the visit is 'for real'.

All this might seem a long way from wanting to *simply* provide a hotline, but considerations such as these can have significant impact; research shows that whistleblowers identify more than twice as much fraud as internal audit, and so the benefits of getting a hotline 'right' should clearly not be underestimated.

Chapter 7: Whistleblowing, Hotlines & Helplines – Testing & What Else?

As highlighted earlier, one issue that deters potential whistleblowers is *fear of the unknown* – again, very real concerns around what will happen, who will know and suchlike. Moreover, further deterrents can be anything perceived by the potential reporter to be an obstacle or delay such that they become nervous, and decide not to make their report. In normal circumstances, they would probably just deal with things, but making a whistleblower report is inevitably perceived as anything but normal.

Many companies launching their new or updated hotline often focus on the posters, policies and communications, etc. that we have already highlighted, without first thinking about how they could genuinely reduce the obstacles, barriers and deterrents to making a report.

Again, companies often treat making a whistleblower report as a transaction when, in reality, it is anything but transactional. Some whistleblowers become hugely distressed in making their report – sometimes delaying doing so until many months after the event, during which time they have wrestled with the potential consequences and have perhaps waited for individuals to move on and away, such that their direct ability to retaliate is at least reduced.

We have already considered making test calls to a company hotline, and I have outlined my personal experience; the seven test reports, including one in school-level French, with the outcome that we only received two of the seven reports, and the handling of the report involving French translation was so appalling and time-consuming that it would have deterred even the most determined reporter.

However, what I previously omitted to say was that of the two calls that were received, only one could be considered as representing a fair record of all the information provided. This is just one example of why calls of this type are only a first step in *genuinely* testing a company hotline.

For example, it is easy to assume that once local in-country hotline phone numbers have been established, then the reports will follow. However, again, it can be imperative to check that those numbers operate, such that a report can definitely be made, including from both landlines and mobile/cell. Moreover, once all that works, what about the hotline and case manager configuration, and the consequent report routing? Beyond that, do all the language facilities operate, and operate well?

Additionally, there are plenty of examples across the world where an employee (or someone else) might make a report 'out of country'; for example, people might work in Switzerland, but live in nearby France where it is arguably less expensive. What would happen if they made their report from France or Switzerland, or indeed, Germany when they are on a business trip – perhaps about an issue that occurred in the Netherlands. Regardless of the details of the locations, small and adjacent countries make this a global issue and so certainly warrants consideration and testing.

One case that I encountered related to a Conflict of Interest involving a company's Chief Finance Officer (CFO), their partner and a six-figure contract. The issue was identified by a whistleblower, but their report was routed to the CFO – who then simply 'sat on it'. The issue was only investigated a year later when the whistleblower resubmitted their report whilst the CFO was on holiday.

This is a further stark example why ongoing 'mystery shopping' or phishing reports to hotlines can be crucial, not only to ensure that there aren't any inadvertent barriers to reporting, but also to test and measure the process end-to-end, from report to case management and on to conclusion and resolution. Clearly, undertaking such 'mystery shopping' needs planning, but it is not onerous to the point that it is practically impossible.

Moreover, if a swathe of employees and others don't feel that they would be supported if they made a report, don't have (for example) work email access, encounter firewalls and a host of other issues in reporting then it is not surprising that that the group will be under-represented in reporting. For this reason, I have found that what is termed **Stand in the Space** can be a crucial approach, whereby a compliance officer (for example) can actually attempt to report and so get to consider and experience a 360-degree view of the full range obstacles, issues and challenges.

Some hotline vendors are starting to implement an 'escrow' capability within their platform for reporting. This means that reporters can still report an issue at, or around, the time that it occurs but it is then held in escrow (i.e. held temporarily) by the platform until the reporter decides that they want it to be reported to their company. This means that the report has the advantage of being contemporaneous, without precluding further information from being added in due course. Crucially, the escrow capability brings benefits for both the reporter and their company; the reporter can be told that *they are not alone* if other similar or related reports are received, such that it gives them confidence to make their report formally. Also, the company could be told that a number of similar reports have been received – without them being given any detail – that they should be aware of, and so can start to take appropriate action.

As we have seen, many companies at the launch, re-launch or refresh of their hotline go into what could be perceived as a fairly standard approach of policies, posters and communications. Whilst these are clearly crucial, there is much more that can be done, done well and done at relatively low cost. For example, at launch run a competition; a competition to, say, make a report about employee restaurant/canteen food; everyone who makes a report gets a modest reward, or is entered in a competition/prize draw.

The competition then serves to familiarise people with the hotline and making a report such that if, and when, they have to make a report 'for real' about an issue or concern, then they are familiar with the process – and the concerns and reservations that they might perceive are reduced. Linked to this is why many companies now try to provide an integrated hotline and helpline, such that there is familiarity and greater ease with the process of both asking a question and making a 'traditional' hotline report. From personal experience of this approach, as we have seen, whilst some reports were definitely hotline and others definitely helpline, there was a surprising level of migration particularly between helpline and hotline, where initial questions turned into something more concerning and serious.

Chapter 8: Retaliation – *the Reality*

It can be easy to assume that retaliation is an employee issue that, should it occur, can be dealt with on a case-by-case basis. However, when people are too afraid to report anything through fear of retaliation then the company loses a crucial source of information – remember that research shows whistleblowers identify more than twice as much fraud as internal audit – and issues continue to fester and increase, people leave, the media perhaps becomes involved and the wider reputation of a company suffers. Retaliation links directly to the culture and trust within a company; if retaliation is allowed to continue unabated then that can prove insidious for a company, but if it is addressed in a way that gives confidence and certainty to employees then everyone – and the company – wins.

Given that, the vast majority of organisations have an 'Anti-Retaliation' or 'No Retaliation' policy for whistleblowers and, without question, such a policy is crucial given that most analyses show fear of retaliation to be the principal reason why employees and others do not make whistleblower reports.

However, most policies are just that; they sit 'on the shelf', are often rarely referred to and may in reality have little impact on what happens day-to-day in a company. Moreover, those policies can range from what is an arguably cursory – but direct – 16 words right through to a standalone policy of 16 or more pages complete with extensive photography and example retaliation scenarios. Regardless of the scope, publishing such a policy is clearly and without question the right thing to do, but the variability in policies is just one indicator of the complexity and challenge of preventing retaliation. Indeed, communication regarding policy and practicalities related to anti-retaliation can be relatively ineffective and limited – often because of a misplaced perception that *retaliation wouldn't really happen here* and, perhaps, a concern over *sowing the seed* regarding retaliatory actions.

However, a policy – short or long – will not prevent retaliation; genuinely preventing retaliation and all its pervasive consequences requires data and analytics to identify and drive compliance and management action. But in practice, many companies and their compliance teams do not really believe that there is the full range of data available to drive an active anti-retaliation programme. As we will see in what follows, that is simply not the case but it requires a perhaps *unconventional* approach.

An array of analyses and reports continue to show that fear of retaliation is by far the most dominant reason why people do not make whistleblower-type reports. Moreover, analysis of the US Equal Employment Opportunity Commission (EEOC) statistics confirm that retaliation remains the most common type of charge filed with the EEOC – yet, staggeringly, retaliation claims are ordinarily the most expensive claims for employers.

Moreover, despite all these anti-retaliation policies, it takes just moments to find appalling cases of retaliation, sometimes involving high-profile and household name organisations, that have taken place on both sides of the Atlantic, and elsewhere – up to and including murder. Not surprisingly, such retaliation can act like a cancer against whistleblowers, and drastically *take the wind out of whistles*.

Companies often find it a challenge to implement comprehensive and effective metrics (Key Performance Indicators (KPIs)) for their compliance and ethics programmes, and the question of metrics becomes even more challenging when it is related to retaliation – particularly so when it comes to proactive measures as opposed to reactive measures; *looking through the windscreen/windshield* to anticipate what could happen as opposed to just *looking through the mirror* at what has already happened. Clearly, however, any and all measures of retaliation are key to achieving an effective anti-retaliation programme in reality.

I would suggest that many, if not most, compliance officers will confirm that, despite their company's anti-retaliation policy, they believe retaliation is alive out in their organisations. The problem is that retaliation can take many forms; it can take place at organisational, manager and colleague level, and involve both *hard* and so-called *soft* retaliation – ranging from discipline, dismissal, harassment, denial of promotion and the loss of a career right through to the *soft* continuous drip-drip of being excluded, not being invited to meetings or social gatherings and incidents of petty spite, such as locker locks being glued and personal belongings being damaged or stolen.

In one case I investigated, a manager made a whistleblower report about bullying by their boss. The ensuing retaliation resulted in the manager experiencing a heart attack – which would have been serious enough of itself had it not been for the fact that the manager's teenage son, fearing that his parent would no longer be able to work and he would have to leave his school, then attempted to commit suicide; retaliation can truly have far-reaching consequences.

In another case, a manager who made a whistleblower report then found almost every day that their allocated parking space was blocked by something. You may say that they were fortunate to have allocated parking, but this was an example of slow but pervasive 'drip-drip' retaliation which consumes the reporter and eventually wears them down. It is arguably a version of gaslighting which is a form of abusive manipulation that makes the reporter (the target) question their judgements, memory, perceptions and reality. Gaslighting is summarised in more detail overleaf.

Retaliation can also take the form of what are termed *micro-retaliations*; generally, a series of retaliations of which individual incidents could – perhaps – be deemed small, minor or inconsequential but taken together represent significant and organised retaliation. Moreover, the continual 'drip-drip' of such micro-retaliations can result in considerable anxiety, distress and unnerving uncertainty and often amplify, such that they become major retaliations.

Put simply, retaliation can take the form of a single *once-and-done* incident, or it can be a series of ongoing incidents, which perhaps involve a variety of forms and perpetrators. Regardless of whether the retaliation involves one or multiple incidents, the result is that the whistleblower becomes unsettled and unnerved as they await the next retaliatory action.

The table shows some specific examples of both types of retaliation, some of which are taken from the EU Whistleblower Protection Directive. It should be stressed that no retaliation is, in reality, 'soft', particularly when it is experienced on a regular and continuing basis.

'Hard' ('Overt') Retaliation	**'Soft' ('Subtle') Retaliation**
Suspension (of all types)	Exclusion from business meetings
Redundancy/lay-off	Exclusion from team meetings
Harm to person or property	Exclusion from social events
Denial of pay rises and/or promotions	Ignored
Harassment	Ostracised ('sent to Coventry' is a British idiom)
Abuse – written/verbal	Professional opinion no longer requested/respected

Implied threat of harm to person or property	Demeaning of work contribution
Biased performance appraisals	Undermining
Reduction in job responsibilities	Humiliation
Reassignment, relocation or transfer	Inferior treatment
Overtime removal/reduction	Pointed 'gossip'
Shift reassignment	Practical jokes/jokes
Removal of company vehicle	Continuing irritations (e.g. car park blocking)
Dismissal (termination)	Rude and disrespectful behaviour
Demotion	Criticism
Withholding of promotion	
Increased workload/extra work	
Post-employment – no, flawed or negative employment references	
Cyber-based attacks etc.	
Social media-based denigration or other harm, including to the person's reputation	
Change of role/responsibilities	
Change of location of place of work	
Reduction in pay and/or allowances	
Changes in working hours	
Withdrawal/withholding of training	
Negative/downgraded performance review	
Disciplinary action/disciplinary penalties including administrative and financial	
Coercion, intimidation or harassment	

Discrimination, disadvantageous or unfair treatment	
Incidents of personal intimidation/violence	
Failure to convert temporary contract into permanent, where there were legitimate expectations that permanent employment would be offered	
Failure to renew, or early termination of, a temporary employment contract	
Financial damage or loss, including loss of business and loss of income	
Blacklisting, informally or formally	
Early termination or cancellation of a contract for goods or services	
Cancellation of a licence or permit	
Medical, psychiatric or other referrals	
Damage to personal property	
Theft of personal property	
'Gaslighting'*	

('Gaslighting' is a more recent phenomena; it is a form of psychological abuse where a person or group makes someone question their sanity, perception of reality or memories. Broadly, it is when one person manipulates another person into questioning their own ability and self-worth. Whilst this most commonly happens in manager-employee relationships, it can happen anywhere regardless of hierarchical structure.)

Whatever form the retaliation takes, it certainly impacts the individual and means that other people will inevitably think twice about whistleblowing.

I became concerned that, in common with most others, a company's anti-retaliation 'toolkit' was both limited and reactive, and essentially relied on training and communications, and investigation and discipline post-event, if indeed it was reported. This situation could not be allowed to continue and I decided to try to take an *unconventional* look at any whistleblower data that there was, and what could be derived; who the whistleblowers were – where that information was available – and then to try to identify data that could potentially indicate retaliation against those individuals. This data for me, as a starting point, included their subsequent annual performance review markings, pay rises, bonuses, disciplinary actions, career progression against their peers, shift allocation and overtime allocation, where appropriate. Not a full or exhaustive set of data, but a subset that I could work with manually to get an indication of whether my retaliation concerns were real or imagined.

It became shockingly obvious within minutes from my simple spreadsheet analysis that retaliation was clearly going on; not everywhere, and not affecting every whistleblower, but it was there. Moreover, some divisions, departments and locations had a noticeably greater propensity for retaliation than others and, I suspected, some of this was linked to certain managers and senior managers. Confirming that issue was largely beyond manual analysis but there were also enough indicators to show that some managers and senior managers essentially *took retaliation with them* when they moved, such that the propensity for retaliation increased. Ascertaining whether this was as a result of command, culture or both would clearly require greater investigation but, regardless, all of this was information that we didn't have prior to starting to undertake relatively simple analysis of data that – crucially – we already had.

Some individuals had clearly been high performers prior to blowing the whistle; after that event – at least if you believed the performance review markings – their performance had declined sharply and, in some cases, had never recovered; a loss to them, and a loss to the company.

Armed with this analysis, it at least enabled me to raise the issue of the *reality of retaliation*, and to get the message out in the company that it was being monitored, however simply and rudimentarily at the time. I would like to think – and there was certainly evidence to this effect – that retaliation lessened to a degree once that message had *done the rounds*, but it can clearly take years for a full pattern to emerge.

However, regardless of its simplicity, this analysis has the potential to deliver multiple benefits; for example, it also enables a 'normalised' range to be established, to see what teams, divisions, countries and suchlike are within and outside those markers. It also enables 'educated' follow-up with whistleblowers to be undertaken, and – as we subsequently discovered – whistleblowers will often come forward with and reveal much more information once they realise that you are coming from a point of (some) knowledge.

On this basis, during our anti-retaliation follow-up with whistleblowers, it was not unusual for the whistleblower to reveal a four- or five-to-one ratio of further retaliation incidents; the analysis might have identified one incident (such as pay), but frequently that was the 'tip of the iceberg' and whistleblowers would reveal several more 'hard' and 'soft' retaliation incidents once they knew you had information and data, and that you weren't going to be fobbed-off such that you went away. Put simply, if a whistleblower had already faced retaliation and you followed-up with them then they would invariably try to get you off the call as quickly as possible, on the basis that they just wanted it all to go away; with information and data to support the follow-up there was a realisation that you were serious, and the situation inevitably changed.

Some readers will say *So what?* on the basis that this is all reactive data – input measures – and the retaliation has happened, such that it is of limited value, and only allows you to *look through the mirror* at the past.

However, that is simply not the case. In reality, once a gathering of retaliation data programme has started, it relatively quickly enables a picture to be built of divisions, departments, locations, teams and role, etc. where there is a propensity for retaliation such that no longer is it purely a case of retrospective data; you can now leverage the data such that you can *look through the windscreen/windshield* proactively and to a degree predictively – and so anticipate what type of location, team, role and report type, for example, usually involved retaliation such that there might be a risk. This then facilitates consideration of what could or is likely to happen, including the propensity for retaliation and its likely type, giving the ability for additional training, communications, reminders and vigilance. Once the programme has started and the data set grows, those input measures can be rapidly turned into output measures, including measures of how effective the anti-retaliation process was. Crucially, this data also enables a far more proactive approach to be taken to anti-retaliation, such that best practice, 'red flags' and suchlike can be actively identified, monitored and managed.

Fear of retaliation is certainly not an issue that is declining, and it remains the dominant reason why employees (and others) do not make whistleblower reports. Some way behind fear of retaliation is a continuing perception or belief that nothing will be done about an issue that is reported, but by regularly publishing anonymised and untraceable whistleblower and retaliation cases, it is possible to communicate some clear messages. Indeed, from personal experience, well-written, interesting, surprising and challenging summaries can become very widely read, and highly respected throughout a company.

For several reasons – including legislative developments – there has been a significant increase in the research, analysis and data available on retaliation and it is interesting to see how some facets of retaliation have arguably changed, for example in relation to the consequences of Covid such as working from home.

The general position is that *internal* reports of retaliation reduced markedly during the times of Covid-19, as a likely result of the phenomena that retaliation reporting declines as people become increasingly concerned about their employment – another manifestation of the fear of retaliation. However, there is arguably a replacement element to this, with *external/third-party* retaliation reporting increasing potentially because of the perception that this approach offers some degree of protection to the reporter.

As one of many, the Ethics and Compliance Initiative (ECI) has undertaken some research in the area of retaliation as part of the data from the Global Business Ethics Survey (GBES). Typically, the ECI research has shown that some 72% of retaliation takes place within three weeks of the report being made and 90% within six months, with the remainder taking place beyond six months.

Clearly, this indicates that whilst the majority of retaliation is reactive and near-immediate (sometimes described as *get mad, get even*), some is deferred to a later date – often to the annual performance review, promotion, pay and/ or bonus rounds, which provide a ready and effective means of retaliation – such that the retaliation can also be potentially disguised within the wider process.

Crucially, this timing of retaliation can cause potential issues regarding data retention, including compliance with the General Data Protection Regulation (GDPR) and some in-country whistleblowing requirements, rules and legislation, given that records of the original whistleblower report could potentially have been deleted prior to the retaliation report being made. This, in turn, can then crucially impact an employer's ability to discharge their Duty of Care responsibilities to employees.

Moreover, employees who make a whistleblower report of wrongdoing may be on heightened alert and perceive a situation or action as retaliation where there is none, or none intended. For this reason, it is important for policies, communications et al. to stress the importance for supervisors and managers to continue to treat a reporter normally following a report. This would clearly include communicating normally, being aware of tone, tenor and body language, ensuring that annual performance reviews are completed without influence, work is allocated objectively, business and social involvement is maintained and, overall, the reporter is treated respectfully whilst also being kept up-to-date on their report. However, in practice, specific anti-retaliation-related training in this regard remains relatively limited and so it remains both a challenge and an opportunity.

Encouraging supervisors and managers such that they ensure retaliation against their team members is prevented and avoided is no easy task, particularly given that retaliation can be the consequence of a wide range of issues. However, done well, anti-retaliation in all its facets can deliver long-term benefit from change in culture. Moreover, there has been some focus on what is sometimes termed *pre-taliation*, which has been variously described as onerous employee non-disclosure agreements that aim to circumvent rules against retaliation and also companies in some way impeding, or detracting from, the ability of a whistleblower to make a report, directly or indirectly. For example, does the company culture demonstrably abhor retaliation, and are there actions and schemes that actively support anti-retaliation?

Following a report, the best whistleblower programmes have a follow-up process, not only to update the reporter on progress (where their identity is known) but also to utilise that opportunity to check for retaliation; clearly, this may therefore require a series of follow-ups extending to several months given that approaching 10% of retaliation occurs more than six months after the original report – which may be well beyond the duration of the report case itself, which would typically be around 40 to 45 days. However, again, the whistleblowing and cultural benefits from such a process should not be underestimated.

Increasingly, whistleblowing platforms are offering a 'scorecard' capability, which aggregates together all of an employees' differing compliance and ethics-related interactions with the platform such as allegations, disclosures, policy attestations and training. Clearly, this gives a good, readily available and 'all-in-one-place' background perspective in relation to whistleblowing and ethical behaviour.

However, going forward, there is the potential to further integrate whistleblower and HR-type data – covering annual performance review markings, pay rises, bonuses, disciplinary actions, overtime awards, recognition, career progression and suchlike – to enable my simple analysis to be turned into an effective real-time compliance tool, such that companies might genuinely experience *No Retaliation* – and be able to prove it, and also be able to readily discharge the retaliation *reverse burden of proof*. This approach was enshrined in the EU Whistleblower Protection Directive but will undoubtedly be adopted more widely, and is considered next.

Companies may consider that they are able to discharge this aspect of the Directive, but I would suggest that it will need to be reviewed and tested, and may ultimately involve a standard anti-retaliation assessment process, weighted on risk such that it considers a range of report-related factors including, as we will see, the potential for *staged retaliation*. Clearly, if the assessment indicated that there was a significant chance of retaliation following a report yet there was no reporter follow-up and no action to ensure and prove that retaliation did not occur – the *reverse burden of proof* – then I would suggest that a company is directly opening itself up to potential issues.

Chapter 9: The EU Whistleblower Protection Directive's *'Reverse Burden of Proof'*

The EU Whistleblower Protection Directive is a good example of leading whistleblowing legislation, which also incorporates some innovative approaches to anti-retaliation; not surprisingly other countries are now starting to consider similar approaches to those enshrined in the Directive, perhaps extending existing legislation in this regard.

Regardless of legislative developments, retaliation can be described as the ***scourge of whistleblowing*** and so companies that are determined to genuinely address retaliation in all its facets may want to enshrine elements of the Directive's approaches in their own policies and practices.

It is important to stress that, for example, the General Data Protection Regulation (GDPR) is a regulation in EU parlance, whereas the EU Whistleblower Protection legislation is a directive. Regulations have binding legal force throughout every EU Member State and become effective on a set date in all the Member States. By comparison, directives lay down certain results that must be achieved but each Member State is free to decide how to transpose them into national laws which has the result (particularly in the case of the Whistleblower Protection Directive) that there are some differences and nuances between the respective Member State implementations, although key principles – such as the *reverse burden of proof* – generally apply universally.

Whatever form retaliation takes, the *Reality of Retaliation* is that it invariably impacts the individual and means that other people will inevitably think twice about whistleblowing – and it was for this type of reason that the

European Commission (EC) introduced for the first time in any legislation a *reverse burden of proof* regarding retaliation within the European Union's (EU) Whistleblower Protection Directive. Under this, it is no longer the responsibility of the whistleblower to prove that they had been retaliated against; it is up to the company or organisation to prove that they *didn't* retaliate – a fundamental and crucial shift in roles and responsibilities, with clear consequences for compliance officers.

Clearly, whilst this is a significant and important step in anti-retaliation, it also brings with it risks, such as the risk of *staged retaliation* where an employee, contractor and suchlike facing legitimate dismissal, an adverse annual review, disciplinary action or loss of contract, for example, lays the foundations for positioning that action as retaliation by making some form of whistleblower report. Put simply, if someone thought they were likely to be dismissed or not receive a bonus or promotion, then a whistleblower report made now might enable them to position that action as retaliation, with all the corresponding legal protections; when they do lose their job or don't get a bonus or promoted, that is their trigger to report it as retaliatory action.

Moreover, in what is a comprehensive piece of legislation, the EU Whistleblower Protection Directive rightly provides protection for a wide range of whistleblowers including, for example, colleagues, supporters and relatives of the reporter. These provisions were included so that, for example, witnesses to an incident reported through the hotline also received the relevant protections. It also serves to address another key risk, that of *indirect retaliation*; indirect retaliation features specifically in the EU Whistleblower Protection Directive and occurs where retaliation against a reporter involves a related party, such as a relative who (say) works at the same company or is a contractor or supplier to that company; indirect retaliation in this way is often used in lieu of direct retaliation against the reporter where that might prove practically and legally problematic. Suddenly, post-report the relative's contract is unexpectedly terminated

– yet indirect retaliation in this way can often go unnoticed and can be difficult to identify given that there is no direct linkage between the reporter and the retaliation. A further variant is where the retaliation is perpetrated by another employee or third party who is in some way beholden to the instigator. It can be easy to assume that this sort of issue wouldn't arise but it is, for example, sometimes prevalent in small and medium cities and towns with a dominant employer – such that whole families have some dependency on that employer, either as employees or suppliers/vendors.

Crucially, the directive also protects a wide range of third-party reporters from retaliation. Such third parties are typically defined as those who are self-employed (contractors), non-executives, volunteers, paid and unpaid trainees, anyone working under the supervision and direction of contractors, subcontractors and suppliers, leavers, job applicants, facilitators and legal entities that the reporter(s) own, work for or are otherwise connected with in a work-related context. As a consequence, the reporting processes necessary to comply with the directive's requirements and to support this group will potentially need to be more extensive and comprehensive, recognising that a legitimate reporter may well never have worked for a company, or may have left many years previously. This is likely, therefore, to involve external publication of reporting numbers, email addresses and suchlike but this then has the potential for those whistleblowing channels to be utilised for customer complaints and similar issues. Clearly, 'turn-back' and 'accept and redirect' are examples of policies that can be adopted, but a policy will need to be considered and decided on.

Many companies have not fully considered or addressed the issue of the EU Whistleblower Protection Directive's *reverse burden of proof*, and will largely still rely on their existing anti-retaliation policy and, perhaps, the mistaken assumption that their incidents of retaliation are not significant. As we have seen, analytics can be crucial here because whilst at the outset, analysis of reports and potential retaliation is all *through the mirror* i.e. reactive and looking backwards at what has happened, over time and with reasonable data volumes, that data can be turned into proactive/predictive *through the windscreen/windshield* i.e. looking forward such that the potential for retaliation based (say) on the type of report, location and other parameters can be assessed, affording the opportunity to consider and take appropriate action. Crucially, it may well be possible to create a standard anti-retaliation assessment process such that for reporters and reports, their *risk of retaliation* is assessed, based on a range of related factors. Whilst this might not prove possible for every report, it could nevertheless be weighted on risk and undertaken for those deemed to be high risk, and could also serve to highlight cases of potentially *staged retaliation*.

As we have previously considered, if the assessment indicated that there was a significant chance of retaliation following a report yet there was no reporter follow-up and no action to ensure and prove that retaliation did not occur – the *reverse burden of proof* – then I would suggest that a company is clearly opening itself up to potential issues.

Overall, the EU Whistleblower Protection Directive has clearly put far greater focus on retaliation with its *reverse burden of proof*. The issue remains that many companies will try to rely largely on what they have now, which will simply not discharge the Directive's requirements, in letter or spirit.

As a simple way of assessing a company's overall preparedness regarding anti-retaliation, and this aspect of the EU Whistleblower Protection Directive, is an *Anti-Retaliation Checklist* which has been included in the Appendices.

Chapter 10: World-class whistleblowing summarised in eight *unconventional* steps

Most companies and organisations face broadly similar concerns and issues regarding whistleblowing. Often, there is a general malaise around whistleblowing, with the result that reporting levels throughout are low, or perhaps in practice largely limited to particular divisions, teams or geographies. Regardless, usually the core questions are how to increase reporting levels in general, and also how to increase reporting from otherwise largely silent parts of a company.

Clearly, increasing reporting levels comes down to what is at the heart of the issue. For example, it could be that supervisors or managers have said to their team something along the lines that *we deal with issues ourselves* with the result that any reticence to report is only compounded. Some readers may say that this sort of thing doesn't happen but, sadly, it does and I have certainly encountered it first-hand.

Step 1: Consider and action potential strategic reasons for low reporting levels

There can be several reasons for low reporting levels, and some nine typical examples are listed here. They include (i) detrimental management actions/statements as outlined above, (ii) concerns over potential retaliation, (iii) lack of awareness about the hotline, knowledge of what it is for and concerns over who can use it, (iv) belief (perhaps from childhood) that you don't *tell the teacher* and therefore you don't report people, (v) belief that nothing will change such that there's no point in reporting, (vi) assumption that someone else would report it (aka *not my business*), (vii) too much bureaucracy to report (aka *too much like hard work*), (viii) thought the company or organisation already knew and/or (ix) a lack of trust in the company.

Having considered the reasons, then it is clearly important to establish an action plan to address them. Some will require more time and effort than others, but many have at their heart *myths*, which need to be dispelled – typically using communications, competitions, feedback, management training, engaging case studies and practical anti-retaliation actions.

Step 2: Consider and action potential practical reasons for low reporting levels

Are low reporting levels universal, or near-universal, throughout the company – or is it confined to particular countries, locations, divisions, teams and suchlike? If so, why? Are the reasons practical, in that telephony or online access is poor, or even non-existent? Are there firewall or telephony quirks? Have you tested your hotline, end-to-end? What about third-party and contractor access?

Social listening, 'pulse' surveys, team meetings, interviews, workshops, manager feedback, contractor meetings and hotline-specific add-ons to company/employee surveys are all examples of opportunities to identify more specific details of why people are not making reports to a hotline.

It might be easy to assume that people have never made a hotline report, but is that the case in reality? Did they perhaps make a report and then encounter inaction, retaliation, obfuscation and lack of conclusion and feedback? If so, is this something that can be identified and addressed?

What is their level of awareness about the hotline, is it readily available to them as outlined above, do they even know it exists and can they readily find out practical details – the details they would need – about it? It might be legally appropriate to have a 27-page whistleblowing policy, but that will be virtually certain to deter potential reporters, or at least cause them to question themselves. Structure and content can be crucial to retaining the reader such that they feel reassured that the hotline is readily available to them, and then confident enough to make a report.

What is their overall level of trust in the company – lack of trust is one of the key reasons why people don't make hotline reports – and what is their level of trust in the hotline itself? Are they confident regarding anti-retaliation, confidentiality and anonymity, and are they also confident that the company will take them seriously, investigate and act? Is the terminology clear and communicated well? Moreover, do they believe that making a report is the right thing to do recognising that, for example, the experiences of people and families in France during World War II subsequently influenced thinking, laws and policies for more than half a century.

Any analytics data that can be ascertained to identify why people are not making hotline reports clearly also has a key role here; where this data doesn't exist, then creating an 'input measure' by, for example, making test reports to a hotline can create crucial and hugely valuable insights. For example, it was only when making a test hotline call that it became evident that the telephony infrastructure in a particular (high-risk) country conspired against such calls, and by not explaining and addressing that, reporting levels were not surprisingly low.

Step 3: Use the analytics, however rudimentary

Put simply, again think about what relevant data there is, or what could be created, and then utilise simple analytics to identify where reports are coming from – and also are not coming from.

If the analytics show low or no reports from particular divisions, teams or geographies then use the analytics as an alert to investigate, understand and re-double communications. It may be that there are genuinely no issues to report, but it could be that reports are actually being suppressed, for a host of reasons.

Step 4: Address 'Fear of the Unknown'

Making a hotline report can be a (very) big step for people, and they will inevitably be fearful of the unknown – such as *What will happen?*, *Who will know?* and, perhaps, *Where will my report go?* Every question like this can result in people deciding not to report and so addressing their 'Fear of the Unknown' can be crucial.

So, use images (of cats, dogs, animals, etc.) to attract people onto the hotline pages, which makes them familiar with the pages whilst also subliminally reassuring/calming them. It can also activate a number of innate processes in people, including smiling and other positive and nurturing behaviours – but research also suggests that images may have an impact on attention and perception. Taking this a step further, if it is possible to change these images periodically, then this provides an additional and continuing 'attraction' to the hotline pages such that if, and when, there comes a time that they do have to use the hotline 'for real', then they are familiar with the pages and the process, such that they are reassured and a 'big step' is a lot smaller in their mind.

When launching the hotline (and periodically thereafter), run a simple competition that invites everyone to make a simple report – on employee restaurant/canteen food, for example; everyone who does so is entered into the competition with the possibility of a prize. In this way, people gain familiarity and reassurance and even if they don't actually make a report, that still stands them in good stead for any future, serious reporting.

Also, unfamiliar terminology can serve to confuse and concern and so also deter. Explain the terminology – 'confidential' and 'anonymous' etc. – which can be confusing, and confusion can result in concerns which again lead to people deciding not to report.

Step 5: Raise awareness
Make your hotline approachable by giving it a brand. Rather than people having 'call the hotline' in their mind with all that entails, branding the hotline *VeRoniCA*, for example (*VeRoniCA* was our Virtual Regulatory Compliance Assistant) opens up multiple possibilities of Ask *VeRoniCA*, *Call Veronica*, etc… This humanises the hotline, gives it an approachable face and reduces the fear of communicating with a nameless function.

Put posters around the offices, sites, plants, etc., including in toilet (washroom) cubicles as they are private, and allow people who are debating whether to call the hotline to read the posters without fear of being seen. At functional level, use tear-off strips on posters (the sort of thing used for second-hand sales etc.) so that people can take hotline contact details with them, not forgetting to tear off a couple of strips at the outset so that people perceive that they are not alone, and their colleagues are also using the hotline. Better still, if budgets allow, include simple credit-card sized 'hotline cards' that people can take with them.

As we have previously touched on, consider how to address every segment of your employee and contractor populations. So, produce a wallet/purse hotline credit card-sized reference for people; analysis shows that once people have these, the resulting retention and awareness rates are very high, for modest investment. If distributing them to every person is logistically challenging or expensive, then leave them out in employee restaurants/

canteens, lifts/elevators and reception areas – the pick-up volume will be surprising, and very valuable. People will still have them in their wallets, purses and work bags even when they are working from home.

Alternatively, try to include hotline details on employee passcards, identity cards and suchlike. Lanyards, pay slips, stickers inside company vehicle windscreens/windshields are further examples of reminders that will potentially be seen regularly, and are inexpensive.

As a further step, produce a 'Z-card' credit-card size version of the Code of Conduct, and include the hotline details on the cover.

People will usually not want to be seen publicly looking at posters, for example – so use special menu cards on employee restaurant/canteen tables to provide a hotline 'ready reference' that can be seen surreptitiously and without issue. Moreover, this approach gives people the opportunity and a little time to read about the hotline.

As a further example of how to address every segment of your employee and contractor populations, if many members of the workforce are, say, involved in external physical work, then put the hotline message on a spectacle cloth – something that they will use several times each day to clean their safety glasses. This is just one example of tailoring the communications channel to sectors of the workforce, particularly those who (may) have a historically low reporting rate.

Some statutory documents will often have to be posted to employees at home; try to get agreement to include hotline information in those types of periodic communication, where their surroundings will likely mean that they are more relaxed about reading it. Send hotline information and reminders periodically via mobile/cell phones, if operationally and legally acceptable.

Recognise that annual employee churn/turnover (for major EU employers) is around 4% per annum – but it is 30% for contractors. As a consequence, hotline awareness for contractors may well need to be undertaken more frequently, and should be reflected in joiner packs and onboarding/induction training.

If possible, identify how many people with a work-based relationship with your company do not have company email addresses or computer access at work. Depending on the results, use some of the techniques in this step to raise hotline awareness within this crucial group, who might otherwise remain uncontacted and unaware.

Use the 'nudge' techniques that we consider subsequently to make the hotline message more compelling. Rather than saying *contact the hotline* use *contact the hotline - other people do* or *contact the hotline – your colleagues do*. This simple change has the potential to deliver noticeable improvements in reporting levels.

Supporting phrases such as *Don't be a bystander*, *If it concerns you, it concerns us* and *See it, Say it, Sort it* can prove to be very compelling and, again, deliver valuable improvements in reporting levels.

Use stories to engage people. Ideally tell anonymised stories of events that have happened in your company, and other companies. Without naming them, use stories to highlight whistleblowers in a positive light and explain how their actions benefited the company and its employees by preventing regulatory issues, fraud, waste, customer loss and similar issues. Respected research continues to highlight how company whistleblowers vastly outperform Internal Audit in identifying fraud – typical figures are that whistleblowers identify more than twice as much fraud – so make use of that type of information and leverage it in your communications.

Have senior management videos produced about the hotline, with a focus on powerful messages about the importance of the hotline to the company, and the responsibilities of individuals to report issues, or concerns. Once produced, these can be utilised in a myriad of ways including links in emails. With so many people currently working from home – full time and part time – posters and employee restaurant/canteen menus, for example, may well not have the reach and value that they previously had. As a consequence, it is important to think about how technology could be deployed to rectify this gap in coverage, and to get the message in front of people; clearly, company wallpapers and screensavers have a potentially key role to play here by incorporating hotline-related messages into what employees see on their work computers.

Similarly, use any workshop and meeting-type opportunities – virtual and in-person – as a vehicle for conveying and reinforcing the hotline message, and provide managers and supervisors with the materials and support to do so. Clearly, it's essential that this is done interactively, and a good example would be a discussion around what could and should be raised via the hotline. From personal experience, using examples of major cases that were raised via a hotline – in your company or, indeed, any company – only serve to reinforce both the importance of the hotline and how a number of these cases were identified by junior employees. Crucially, anything hotline-related of this nature needs to be fun and engaging, and good examples will lead to good discussions. The shop worker who complained via the hotline about his work snacks being stolen that led onto a major drugs investigation never fails to surprise and engage…!

Recognise that Covid-19 and working from home may have affected a number of wider issues, including hotline reporting levels, hotline awareness and compliance, particularly as people became increasingly concerned about keeping their jobs. Use return-to-work-type communications, reminders and briefings (including Zoom/Teams calls) to raise hotline awareness.

As we have already seen, the EU Whistleblower Protection Directive, for example, supports hotline reporting from a wide range of third-party reporters and protects them from retaliation. Such third parties are typically defined as those who are self-employed (contractors), non-executives, volunteers, paid and unpaid trainees, anyone working under the supervision and direction of contractors, subcontractors and suppliers, leavers, job applicants, facilitators and legal entities that the reporter(s) own, work for or are otherwise connected with in a work-related context. As a consequence, the reporting processes necessary to comply with the directive's requirements and to support this group will potentially need to be more extensive and comprehensive, recognising that a legitimate reporter may well never have worked for a company and just went through the recruitment process, or may have left many years previously. This is likely, therefore, to involve external publication of reporting numbers, email addresses and suchlike – perhaps within supplier and vendor portals or even on the company website – but this then has the potential for those whistleblowing channels to be utilised for customer complaints and similar issues. Clearly, this is an issue that can be addressed, but it is nonetheless important to be aware of.

Conversely, don't fall into the traps. It might seem like an obvious idea to put an onsite hotline postbox in your offices or plants – and it might be – but will it get used? How will people feel about the risk of being seen using it? Careful positioning of the postbox could make all the difference by balancing easy access with discretion. Given its relative ease of implementation, just one report received in this way would arguably make it worthwhile and so the approach might well be worth some experimentation, particularly, for example, if the local workforce isn't readily able to get online at work.

Step 6: Genuinely and practically address fear of retaliation

It doesn't take much research to discover absolutely horrendous stories of retaliation, and also its often unseen consequences. From the 'drip-drip' of what are sometimes termed *micro-retaliations*, such as daily blocking of a reporter's car parking space right through to murder, attempted suicide and suchlike.

It is for this reason that any company whistleblowing programme that aspires to be world-class has to address retaliation, using practical steps not just a well-intended 'shelf policy'. Moreover, the risk of retaliation is such that whistleblowing laws around the world – including the EU Whistleblower Protection Directive – are increasingly incorporating anti-retaliation requirements.

Clearly, it is essential to stress from the outset how your company utilises confidentiality and anonymity regarding the hotline, as just two of a number of protections afforded to whistleblowers. It is also essential to stress that 'everyone is treated equally' as part of the principle of what is termed 'organisational justice'.

The concept of organisational justice relates to employee perceptions of fairness in the workplace and how employees judge the behaviour of the organisation, and the employees' resulting attitude and behaviours. If, for example, an employee feels a sense of injustice then that will invariably result in a change in attitude and a consequent drop in engagement, productivity and overall performance.

As a consequence, it is essential to ensure that organisational justice operates with the company, and is also seen to operate – such that everyone is treated equally and held to the same standards, regardless of whether they are *top-floor, shop floor* or favoured high performer. Bringing home this message can often be achieved through anonymised stories of executives and suchlike being held to account.

An absolute law can be defined as a code for human conduct that is derived from the morals that should be universal to all human beings and, for this reason, it is important to communicate and stress the absolute nature of your anti-retaliation policy. This can be supported by examples of some of the active measures and checks and balances that are undertaken to monitor – and prevent – retaliation whilst also consistently and continuously reinforcing the message at local workshops and events that retaliation in any form will not be tolerated.

Convey the key message of *Report & Support,* i.e. make a report and you will be supported. Most advice on preventing retaliation hinges on periodic/regular follow-up with reporters. However, to do this well needs the *Reality of Retaliation* to be taken into account. For example, unprepared follow-up with a reporter will often result in them not admitting to having faced retaliation, because they simply want it all to 'go away'. Not only will they not engage properly regarding this report, it probably makes it unlikely that they will ever make a report again – and that message will get out to friends and colleagues such that this one failure regarding retaliation will have multiple consequences.

As we have seen, it is essential to use simple analytics to see what happened to the reporter's career, pay, promotion, annual review, overtime, shift allocation, etc. post-report, and use this in the follow-up. Armed with this information such that you are coming from a position of knowledge will make all the difference. You can turn a flat denial in response to the question *Have you faced any problems or retaliation?* into a dialogue – valuable to both parties – regarding their report, and what happened subsequently. Questions such as *Do you know why your annual review marking was lower this year following your report?* and *Do you know why you were moved to the nightshift a few weeks after your report?* can elicit surprising responses, often because the reporter has had nowhere to go and has, crucially, lost faith in 'organisational justice'. From personal experience, going in to these reporter follow-ups from a position of supposed knowledge often resulted in a four- or five-to-one 'multiplier effect', i.e. you might suspect one incident of retaliation, but the reporter will often reveal more. Put simply, getting the reporter engaged in this way using knowledge of one potential retaliation incident will often elicit reports of four or five other incidents – for example *I'm not invited to team meetings now*, *I'm ignored by my manager* or *Things get stolen from my desk.*

It is crucial to recognise that reporter follow-up is not something that is *once-and-done*, so the process will need to be properly planned, managed and executed. As we have already considered, reporter follow-up needs to be undertaken regularly after their report, given that some retaliation can be subtle, and undertaken over a long period.

The Ethics & Compliance Initiative (ECI) has identified that, broadly, some 72% of retaliation occurs in the three weeks following a report being made, and 90% within six months. This means that anything up to 10% of retaliation occurs more than six months after the report, and so reporter support is clearly not a 'once-and-done' activity. Early retaliation can take many forms but is clearly an opportunistic, immediate reaction so may be less well planned. Later retaliation could be described as planned or synchronised retaliation, although it can be just apathy that delays the retaliation, or an eventual realisation that the report and its contents are serious. As an example, planned retaliation can be synchronised with the annual pay, bonus or promotion round, such that the reporter is disadvantaged but the retaliation is disguised and 'lost' within that wider process.

It is also important to recognise the potential for other relation-related phenomena that we have considered earlier including what is termed 'indirect retaliation', and also 'staged retaliation'.

Indirect retaliation features directly in the EU Whistleblower Protection Directive and occurs where retaliation against a reporter involves a related party, such as a partner who, say, works at the same company or is a contractor to that company. Retaliation in this way can often go unnoticed and can be difficult to identify given that there is no direct linkage between the reporter and the retaliation.

Staged retaliation is where, say, an employee fears that they will lose their job, not get promoted, have an adverse annual review, etc. and so makes some report such that when they do lose their job or don't get promoted, they position it as retaliation.

Many companies have not fully considered or addressed the issue of the EU Whistleblower Protection Directive's *reverse burden of proof*, and are largely still relying on their existing anti-retaliation policy and perhaps the mistaken assumption that their incidents of retaliation are not significant. Analytics can be crucial here because whilst at the outset, analysis of reports and potential retaliation is all 'through the mirror', i.e. reactive and looking backwards at what has happened, over time and with reasonable data volumes, that data can be turned into proactive/predictive 'through the windscreen/windshield', i.e. looking forward such that the potential for retaliation based, say, on the type of report, location and other parameters can be assessed, affording the opportunity to consider and take appropriate action. Crucially, it may be possible to create a process such that for each reporter and report, their *risk of retaliation* is assessed; whilst this might not prove possible for every report, it could nevertheless be undertaken for those deemed to be high risk, and could also serve to highlight cases of potentially staged retaliation.

Overall, the EU Whistleblower Protection Directive has clearly put far greater focus on retaliation with its 'reverse burden of proof'. The issue remains that many companies will try to rely largely on what they have now, which will simply not discharge the Directive's requirements, in letter or spirit.

As a simple method of assessing a company's overall preparedness regarding anti-retaliation, and this aspect of the EU Whistleblower Protection Directive, an 'Anti-Retaliation Checklist' has been included in the Appendices.

Step 7: Address cultural barriers to whistleblowing (aka *It's not for me* or *We do not do that here*)
In some cultures and countries, moments in history – such as World War II – have shaped the perception of whistleblowers, and whistleblowing; these perceptions are only now changing more than half a century on, often in

response to international legislative developments.

If there is the potential for cultural issues such as these, then it is important for companies to get *on the front foot* and share messaging from colleagues and senior managers promoting the hotline. Crucially, the messaging can be around protecting the company – not the one or two people involved in the theft, fraud, harassment or other issue, but the thousands of people whose livelihoods would be threatened directly or indirectly if the company was damaged (or destroyed) by the actions of the few bad apples.

It is also important to communicate examples of how people are using the hotline and speaking up so that it is not seen as unusual or isolated. It can be valuable to support these examples with employee survey results; for example, *90% of our employees stated that if they saw something out of the ordinary, they would report it*. Alternatively, hotline metrics can be very powerful, such as the company having 60 issues or concerns raised through the hotline every month – which, broadly, means that some 700 people annually are using, and engaging with, the hotline. Whatever the purpose and values of the company, those are important and need to be protected – and the hotline can be readily positioned as supporting that.

Again, use local workshops, events and suchlike to raise awareness of the importance of raising concerns. There are wide-ranging and powerful of examples of where, for example a minor failure to report an issue can later result in major consequences, and these can really bring home the hotline/reporting messages to people, often for the first time.

Step 8: Ensure people know their concerns will be taken seriously
People often don't report concerns because they do not believe that their concern will be addressed, or they will be thought of as making a fuss or something similar. Stress that reports will be investigated and, as long as they are made in good faith, there will be no detriment to the reporter. Again, regularly share stories in a newsletter or similar that will likely be read throughout the

company of how cases have been reported, investigated and those involved held accountable.

Clearly, the performance of both hotline intake and case management are crucial, and all elements will affect how the hotline is perceived and used. Well-managed and structured intake channels, for example, can serve to greatly reduce the emotional and functional barriers to optimise and humanise the whistleblowing experience.

Clearly, it is important to investigate cases efficiently whilst keeping the reporter informed on progress and conclusion, recognising that confidentiality and other sensitivities may mean that the reporter is not able to be given full details. These make the reporter feel that their concern is being taken seriously and, again, they will undoubtedly share this within the company – which also serves to build a reputation for care, concern, efficiency, empathy, confidentiality and diligence.

It can certainly be worth testing and analysing what happens after a report has been received, including the process performance, and also the 'tone' and perception of subsequent communications and interactions. These can make all the difference as to how the hotline is perceived, with all the consequences for future reporting levels that will bring.

From personal experience, annual (anonymised) compliance and ethics reports can have a key role here, with a hotline/discipline-related subset published internally which demonstrates reports are investigated, and actions taken up to and including dismissal/termination. Interest in the cases can prove to be a driver of interest in the wider report, and compliance and ethics more generally.

Chapter 11: *The Corporate Shield*: What's your Compliance & Ethics *Shield*?

What keeps your company compliant and ethical? What are the activities, processes, controls and systems that make up your company's compliance and ethics programme, and do they join-up? How would you know, and how would you evaluate them?

In reviewing and reflecting on a company's compliance and ethics programme one day, I wanted to know in simple terms what protected that company; what the company had in place that *shielded* them from compliance and ethics failures, and kept them away from the fines, reputational damage and other consequences that come from such a failure.

It was a simple concept, and one that everyone understood very quickly, and the reasoning behind it. From that concept, ultimately came the *Corporate Shield* – a simple pictorial and practical representation of a company's compliance programme, which can be used to identify the compliance and ethics activities, processes, controls and systems that are in place, their performance and the gaps – those that *should* be in place. The simplicity of the Corporate Shield template is illustrated here on the next page.

Some readers would probably argue that their company already has a well-managed risk register process, and through that they identify and analyse their compliance and ethics risks, develop response plans and assign responsibilities such that the risks are (progressively) mitigated. However, not every company operates such a process and, in any case, the compliance and ethics-specific elements are often limited, and insufficiently granular. Moreover, the risk register process can sometimes be deemed to be a chore and 'tick-the-box' rather than something that really engages, gets people thinking and provides a more immediate 'living' view of the broader compliance and ethics capabilities – and omissions and gaps – in a company.

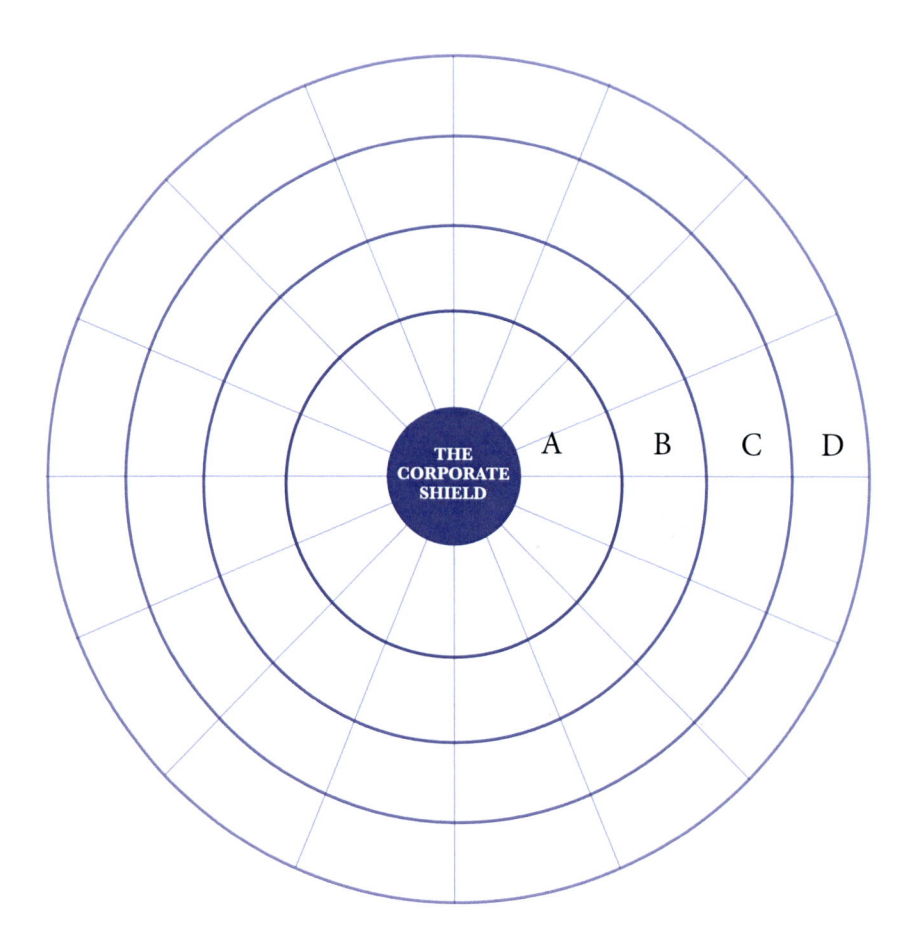

THE CORPORATE SHIELD   A   B   C   D

Against that, the Corporate Shield can be used by individuals, small groups and teams within a company, division or function and also provides the facility for a quantitative analysis of an overall compliance programme, and its individual elements – which invariably delivers some surprising results, as we will see in a moment. The quantitative analysis may be quick and simple, but it is nonetheless very effective and also provides the platform for valuable comparative assessments.

I have used it internationally with a range of audiences at a variety of workshops and events and it is always well-received, and always proves to be an eye-opener for delegates. Crucially, it can be completed quickly or slowly – from less than 30 minutes end-to-end or 90 minutes-plus where the desire is to facilitate in-depth debate around the analysis and resulting issues.

Briefly, the first step in the process is simply to identify the elements of what your company's Corporate Shield is made up of, including existing elements, and those that are aspired to. There are 16 boxes in the outer circle 'D', which are used to record each element, activity, process, etc. of a compliance and ethics programme that shield and protect the company, organisation, division, subsidiary or activity (such as a call centre).

Examples of those elements, activities, processes, etc. could include training, communications, whistleblowing, codes, policies, disclosures and audit together with (perhaps) specific processes regarding competition law (anti-trust), Anti-Bribery & Corruption (AB&C), data privacy, Conflict of Interest, anti-retaliation and so on.

I almost always see at least ten and, more often, all 16 boxes completed – and quite often delegates, colleagues, etc. will list more on another sheet. Moreover, regardless of whether the Corporate Shield is completed by individuals, small groups or teams, it will lead to debate, which only serves to support engagement, learning, review and comparisons.

Circle 'C' is then used to quickly rate each of the elements (entries) in circle 'D' in terms of *importance* to the compliance programme, using a simple 1, 2, 3, 4 or 5 rating scale where '5' is high importance and '1' is low. Similarly, circle 'B' is then used to rate each of the entries in circle 'D' in terms of current *performance*, using a similar scale where '5' is high performance and '1' is low.

As an example, whistleblowing could be deemed highly important to a company and so would warrant a '5' rating in 'C' – but the company performance in relation to whistleblowing might be considered poor and so this might result in a '1' or, perhaps, '2' rating in 'B'. Clearly, this rating process will again lead to debate, engagement, comparison and review.

If, for example, a Conflicts of Interest process was deemed very important to a company but, for some reason, it didn't have one in place then this might well lead to a high rating of '5' for Importance, but, clearly, a very low rating of '1' for Performance.

Finally, circle 'A' is then used for a simple subtraction for each entry based on the ratings in 'B' and 'C' for each entry, retaining any minus signs – which would be the situation where the rating for Importance in 'C' is less than the rating for Performance in 'B'. So, for that same Conflicts of Interest process, the overall quantitative analysis rating might be '4' – based on a rating of '5' for Importance but only '1' for Performance. As a further example, in the event – perhaps unlikely – that the Conflicts of Interest process was rated as '3' for Importance and '4' for Performance, then the overall quantitative analysis rating would be '-1'.

What the results in 'A' lead to is that those elements that have the greatest numerical gaps between 'B' and 'C' are those where there is the greatest requirement – and opportunity – for improvement, because whilst Importance is high, Performance is rated as low; the bigger that numerical gap, the greater the opportunity.

However, where the numerical gaps between 'B' and 'C' are negative, this means that Importance is low but Performance is rated as high. Put simply, this means that your company is very good at the things that don't matter, or matter less, such that the effort currently invested in those could be reinvested into other activities that have greater importance; it is this aspect that invariably proves to be a genuine eye-opener for delegates.

Crucially, although what has been described here is a top-level or overall analysis, a 'Russian Doll'-type approach to the Corporate Shield can be used to drill down further to provide more granular, detailed results for specific element(s) of the overall shield; for example, if whistleblowing is a key element of the overall shield, then the shield approach can be applied specifically to whistleblowing, and all the elements of that, such as telephony, intake, case management and suchlike.

The Corporate Shield template with instructions is also included in the Appendices.

Chapter 12: *How far would you go?* Conventional – and *unconventional* – compliance: *Mystery Shopping* and *Phishing*

How far would you go – within the law and reasonable norms of behaviour – to develop, deliver and maintain your company's compliance programme? This was the question that I posed to myself – as part of *leaving no stone unturned* – and have subsequently regularly posed to compliance and ethics teams and event audiences. How far would you go?

Virtually every compliance officer sees and uses phrases around 'achieving world-class compliance' – but how far would you go in order to deliver that objective given that the *conventional* techniques available to compliance officers in practice are, arguably, limited? There are the 'usual suspects' such as training, communications and analytics (perhaps) but beyond those, what effective levers, in reality, does a compliance officer have? Could – and should – compliance officers utilise phishing-type and mystery/secret shopping stimulus-response approaches in order to test the wider compliance and ethics performance of their company? Moreover, where does this move over the boundary line from acceptable business practice to protect a company into something else? Again, how far would you go?

The first step for a compliance officer is to really identify and analyse the practical risks in their compliance and ethics programme. Many companies have well-developed risk analysis processes and the risks associated with their compliance and ethics programme may well be identified as part of that; however, I would suggest that at group or company level, the compliance and ethics risks identified may not be sufficiently granular such that the compliance officer will need to identify the detailed risks and formulate their responses; the *Compliance & Ethics Shield* in my view is a very useful tool in this regard, which supports a straightforward, consultative and multi-stakeholder perspective that provides both a qualitative and simple quantitative analysis.

It is (relatively) easy to keep rolling-out training and communications, for example, as stalwarts and key tools in the compliance officer's armoury in order to provide a risk response. However, regardless of how good the training content, visual appeal, games and messaging tone are, they will arguably not have the ongoing impact to make employees really sit up and take notice; what would you do to achieve that objective?

What follows are just some examples of 'how far would you go' – *unconventional*, effective and valuable ways to push the boundaries of what might be deemed *conventional* compliance. They bring risks, but they also bring the potential for genuine and long-term impact.

Compliance-by-mail – **the 'bottle-shaped box'** Companies may very occasionally make the decision to send an important compliance-related booklet, report or pamphlet through the mail. Whilst there are clearly environmental considerations, this is one approach that can be used to address hard-to-reach employee, contractor and other groups that, for example, do not have access to company email, and can also serve to provide a degree of differentiation and impact for those employees who do have company email but where this type of compliance-related communication might be lost or ignored in the myriad of daily emails. Whilst this approach can be expensive and does not necessarily guarantee delivery to the individual, it is *different* and so there may be resulting benefits in terms of awareness and learning.

However, in considering the advantages and disadvantages of *compliance-by-mail*, it made me think of what could be sent that would be potentially tailored to specific audiences (employee groups) and have genuine impact, far in excess of what might be perceived as 'routine' training.

One example that proved particularly effective was to send a low-cost bottle-shaped box to everyone in the procurement team at Christmas which, rather than what they expected, contained a copy of the Gifts & Hospitality (Gifts, Travel & Entertainment) policy. It was something that the team probably never forgave me for, but they also never forgot it and so the long-term impact – measured, for example, in increased levels of disclosure – was both significant and sustained, and achieved at very modest real cost.

Gifts & Hospitality/Gifts, Travel & Entertainment *'apathy'*
Companies often apply considerable effort into establishing and communicating Gifts & Hospitality (Gifts, Travel & Entertainment) programmes and policies, which can be complex and extensive particularly where international operations are involved. Companies sometimes also implement a range of associated processes, such as the laudable facility to declare (disclose) and raffle any business gifts received and then donate the proceeds to charitable causes. As part of their processes, many companies produce extensive records and analytics to try to ensure, for example, that country gift rules and thresholds have been complied with, given that those are likely to feature in any regulatory-type investigation.

So far, so good. However, the problem comes that whilst not perfect, gifts and hospitality given (*outbound*) can often largely be controlled and reconciled through the expenses process, but there is no comparable control and reconciliation of gifts and hospitality received – the *inbound* side. If someone forgets or wantonly decides not to make a declaration then it will often largely go unnoticed; there have been a number of international court cases where the provision Gifts & Hospitality was clearly undertaken on an 'industrial' scale – but it must have started somewhere.

It was this issue that triggered me to think about whether, in the absence of a reconciliation, there could at least be some form of alert process regarding inbound hospitality that would also serve to make clear the situation was being monitored.

One example of what came from this for me was an analysis of lunchtime and late afternoon supplier/vendor visits to the main sourcing/procurement offices derived from the visitor and door entry logs, on the basis that – given the timings – there was a high likelihood that (at least) a lunch, dinner or meal of some type would be involved, and potentially other gift-giving. The analysis only served to reveal a pattern of significant under-reporting of hospitality which, although not perfect, provided some useful analytics, and the basis for other, similar approaches.

Compliance training and *'Phishing'* As we consider elsewhere, many compliance and ethics-related measures are *input* measures and, arguably, accurate and effective *output* measures of compliance and ethics are more difficult to identify, establish and maintain.

Compliance and ethics-related training is a good example, where the measures invariably relate to inputs – such as course completions, usually both in absolute and percentage terms *(73 people, 97.8% of the sales team have completed their compliance and ethics training)*. Again, so far so good – but the corresponding *output* measure of the benefits of the training can clearly be far harder to assess.

However, given the importance and potential value of a corresponding output measure, would you go as far as *creating* such a measure? Would you use phishing-type techniques – a type of social engineering where a message is designed to elicit (and in this case, test) a response from a person?

In one example, some 1,435 employees out of a population of 1,500 completed their Anti-Bribery and Corruption training; given those numbers, all the *input* measures were good, with a near-96% completion rate. However, six months on would you send a fictitious letter to those 1,435 employees inviting them and their families to an all-expenses paid *day at the races*? Astonishingly, about 15% of the recipients accepted without question, and another 10% responded along the lines of 'I would have attended, but you didn't give enough notice'!

Some readers might consider this approach to be unacceptable behaviour – 'trickery' or entrapment, perhaps – but what it did serve to do was change an often passive 'tick-the-box' approach to Anti-Bribery & Corruption training (essentially, 'I attended') into something with more active engagement and awareness. However, the other side of that coin is that someone I know completed their compliance training but, by their own admission, spent most of the time scrolling through work emails. Ultimately, that person spent time in prison, their company was fined and also incurred substantial costs because of a compliance failure related to the very compliance training that they had been through, and that is one reason why *how far would you go?* remains a crucial question for me.

Conflicts of Interest As part of their wider governance processes, some companies periodically run comparisons between the employee bank accounts on their payroll, and the bank accounts on their master third-party/supplier/vendor listing. Clearly, this can be used (with limitations) to identify common bank accounts, and company employees who are also suppliers to the company; whilst there might be reasons for this, I would suggest that it is invariably an eye-opener.

On a similar principle, provided that it is within local privacy, employment and related laws, it is often possible to research and identify employees who are also registered in a director or in a similar role in a company or organisation, and also where their home addresses are recorded as a registered company office; the company registered at their home address may have nothing to do with them, but in my experience, such comparisons can often throw up hitherto unidentified and questionable issues. Clearly, a Google search may identify further external roles which can all then be compared to their Conflicts of Interest disclosure, if they have made one; if they haven't then there is the opportunity to, potentially, use the research to request a disclosure. Such research can be time-consuming and so will likely be restricted to those employees and others that are deemed to be high risk, for whatever reason. Equally clearly, some companies may deem this approach unacceptable, too intrusive or even perhaps illegal, but it does potentially offer the opportunity to identify certain Conflicts of Interest. Crucially, however, communicated well, it makes clear that the process is not passive and that their employer is following up, even if their outside appointment does prove to be innocuous.

Mystery shopping Utilised ethically, mystery shopping can be a valuable way of measuring key aspects of a company's performance across a raft of activities, including quality of sales and service and job performance – and also regulatory compliance.

It is a common technique used in a range of sectors, but using it in a regulatory compliance *assurance* role outside financial services is relatively rare. It is a tool that compliance officers could use, but often don't, because its potential value and relevance to their programme is just not fully considered.

An issue over the compliance performance of call centres which could have resulted in a company ending up in court, triggered me to think about how we could far better measure our compliance performance using approaches taken from other industries and applications; the thoughts that kept coming into mind were (i) *mystery shopping* and (ii) *stimulus-response*, i.e. an approach that measured compliance performance in response to a scenario stimulus or issue.

Put simply, the mystery shopping programme was a revelation. It served to identify common compliance failures and enabled a wider *stimulus-response* approach to be deployed, such that specialist scenarios could be tested. Moreover, root-cause analysis provided a rich source of compliance assurance, and directly relevant measures.

Overall, mystery-shopping-type approaches, whilst not universally applicable to all aspects of compliance, nonetheless represent potentially vital, *unconventional* and much under-used techniques in the compliance officer's toolkit.

Chapter 13: The Cost of Compliance & Other *Unconventional* Leadership Opportunities

I doubt that there are many compliance professionals who haven't encountered (and struggled with) the perennial issue of *engaging the board*. Engaging the board (and other senior teams) is clearly crucial; not only will an engaged board support a compliance and ethics programme and the compliance and ethics team, but it will also set the right 'Tone-at-the-Top', with all the benefits that brings. Moreover, an engaged board will also support the Chief Compliance and Ethics Officer should the need arise, particularly where independence is required.

However, the reality can be that engaging with your board can be a challenge. From personal experience, one board member was entirely supportive and fully engaged with compliance and ethics. However, their successor was at the other end of the spectrum and gained the unfortunate nickname of *five times*, because every time we booked a meeting with them, it would usually then be cancelled five times!

The relationship between compliance and the board is sometimes described as having a *saw-tooth* pattern or a *half-life* – a term describing radioactive decay; a crisis incident occurs, the board becomes engaged, complains that they weren't aware, the issue gets resolved and then, progressively, the board's engagement decays until the next major crisis. Regardless of how it is described, this scenario is clearly far from ideal in maintaining board engagement and, indeed, avoiding those major crises in the first place.

Whilst there is a plethora of material around regarding 'building better board engagement' and suchlike, that material rarely refers to *destroying the myths* of compliance and ethics. For example, talk to the majority of people in a company, including board members, and I would suggest that they will almost inevitably believe that effective compliance and ethics comes at a high price – certainly a high price compared to the perceived risk, both financial and non-financial. Clearly, this is mostly based on perceptions, supported by increasingly high-profile headlines about compliance, new legislation and the associated costs to business.

However, do you genuinely know what your company's *Cost of Compliance* is – and, if you did, how could you use that data to start to *destroy the myths* that surround compliance in general and your company's compliance and ethics programme specifically?

I decided that I simply wanted to understand what the independently audited cost of compliance might be, how that compared with a few other companies and whether I could satisfy myself that it represented value for money. For simplicity, I defined the 'Cost of Compliance' as spend per employee per annum on compliance such that it could be normalised and thereby offer generally valid comparisons; it didn't need to be accurate to multiple decimal places, but it did need to be audited and traceable.

To put the cost of compliance in context, it will take you moments to find household-name companies and organisations that have been fined for compliance failures, such as competition law (anti-trust) offences; as examples, one company was fined the equivalent of £1,380 (approximately $1,650) per employee, another £1,630 ($1,950) and another £1,035 ($1,250). Clearly, these are just single fines and do not preclude the potential for further fines related to subsequent compliance failures.

By comparison, companies that I have worked with would manage their programmes such that the level of compliance and ethics investment spend was around £10 to £22 ($12 to $27) per employee per annum. By comparison, the fines above represent some 150 times that figure – and to put £10 to £22 in perspective, it equates to just a couple of trips on the Underground (subway) in London.

I readily accept that this is not a sophisticated comparison, yet what it does indicate is that a compliance programme costing £10 to £22 per employee per annum appears to offer good value and clear benefit when compared against the fines (alone) that could result from a compliance failure; the legal, reputational, management and other costs that invariably arise from a compliance failure would only serve to improve the cost-benefit analysis.

Even if you question the hypothesis of *relative* compliance cost – the relativity of annual compliance costs and typical fines normalised on a per-employee basis – the use of *absolute* compliance costs, i.e. the cost of compliance per employee per annum, is still a potentially crucial measure regarding the performance and development of your compliance programme. If you haven't assessed what your current level of spend (investment) is, then I'd suggest you get it assessed – ideally, independently – and then consider what opportunities, benefits and risks would potentially arise from a spend of, say, 10% more – and also 10% less. Your budget amortised over the number of employees may be a good starting point, but invariably some compliance-related costs are taken elsewhere in a company with the result that budget and actual expenditure may differ. Regardless, understanding your company's *Cost of Compliance* and thinking about its positioning and presentation can prove to be a very powerful tool in the compliance officer's armoury, and in engaging the board.

The plethora of material around regarding 'building better board engagement' contains an array of advice around presentation, data, financial analysis, tools, spreadsheets, timings and demonstrating effectiveness and, clearly, building a relationship with the board crucially depends on these, but also *destroying the myths*. However, an experiment that I undertook invited people, including the most senior, to suggest how much as a company we spent on compliance. Some of those responses were *more than ten times the reality* and so it is reasonable to think that these people's thinking and perception could well have been skewed, such that it had the potential to affect their personal engagement, perceived risk assessment and value analysis.

The *Cost of Compliance* is a question that I have raised regularly at international compliance, legal and related events yet, to date, I have only ever encountered one delegate who responded with a comparative figure. That is the sum total of my responses, which implies that many compliance and ethics officers are missing an opportunity to consider, manage and position their company's compliance and ethics investment in this way – and also positively demonstrate the value of their programme (and their own value) to the company.

Chapter 14: Compliance & Ethics
Nudge – and *Sludge*
Using nudge to budge compliance & ethics: How small changes can deliver big benefits

Nudge theory is a concept in behavioural science that brings together understanding of how people think, positive reinforcements, reduction of unhelpful influences and indirect suggestions in order to influence the behaviour of individuals or groups. Nudge theory is utilised to shape thinking and decision-making whilst allowing an individual to retain freedoms of choice and, hence, feel in control of the decisions that they make.

Whilst nudge theory should be a crucial approach in delivering compliant and ethical behaviour, in reality it is a much under-used technique in the compliance officer's toolkit, particularly when compared with other tools and techniques available to compliance officers, such as training, education and enforcement. The *concept of nudge* first came to public attention in the early 2000s and since then, several 'nudge units' have been established, including one by the UK government.

As an example, changing *Take Your Litter Home* – a sign seen widely throughout the UK for many years – to *Take Your Litter Home Other People Do* resulted in markedly increased levels of compliance, and represents a good example of what nudge theory can offer, at minimal cost and complexity. Most compliance officers will have written something around *Complete Your Compliance Training* at some point, but what might be the impact in your company of changing it to *Complete Your Compliance Training – Your Colleagues Do*; crucially, the cost and time involved would be virtually negligible.

Image: Courtesy of Tonbridge & Malling Borough Council/Lunatic Laboratories

Similarly, a trial with Her Majesty's Revenue & Customs (HMRC) – the UK equivalent of the US Internal Revenue Service (IRS) – showed how telling late taxpayers that most people in their towns had already paid their tax increased payment rates by some 15 percentage points. Similarly, a trial with the UK's Courts Service showed how personalised text messages were six times more effective than final warning letters at prompting fine payments. Moreover, in one trial, a letter sent to non-payers of vehicle taxes was changed to use plainer English, along the lines of 'pay your tax or lose your car'. Just rewriting the letter in this way doubled the number of people paying the tax.

As this shows, simple changes in language and presentation can have very marked effects on results. Research into why people did not take up financial incentives to reduce energy consumption by insulating their homes found that one key issue was the effort, disruption and clearing involved. Addressing issues such as this – *Sludge* – which bog people down, led to a three-fold increase in take up by using a simple process nudge. Crucially, removing the sludge was far more effective than anything else, including bigger financial subsidies.

Delivering effective communications is a key component of any compliance and ethics programme, yet is one of the perennial challenges for virtually every compliance officer, irrespective of industry and geography; it is a challenge because implementing an effective communications regime hinges on a host of interconnected issues, including messaging frequency, volume, complexity, channels and tailoring, plus effective stakeholder management.

Moreover, whilst there is plenty of material around on 'effective compliance communications', there is relatively little that details the principal three communications routes – direct, indirect and subliminal – that organisations can use to deliver compliance communications. Typical examples of these routes would be email (direct), poster campaigns (indirect) and compliance branding (subliminal); as we have seen, branding our compliance hotline as *VeRoniCA* – our Virtual Regulatory Compliance Assistant – had the result that not only did it remove the usual perceptions of hotlines and reporting, but it also opened up a whole series of other communications opportunities, such that *Ask VeRoniCA* came into common company parlance.

Most compliance communications are written in the language that comes to us the easiest – *business speak* – and are prepared largely generically for a company-wide audience. For a compliance team, this approach often means that something can be written, stakeholders (legal, HR and others) involved get it agreed and then it can be simply sent out; job done!

Unfortunately, it often wasn't; it can quickly become evident that a communications programme is simply not effective – often based on both anecdotal and factual evidence. For example, many communications can be largely ignored, skim-read at 4.55 pm on a Friday night or, worse still, deleted without reading. In truth, often-held perceptions of compliance can mean that any related communications need to be powerful, compelling and stand out, often just in order to achieve what is a simple objective.

I'm sure those issues are familiar to many people reading this but, as a consequence of that type of evidence, 'nudge' has to be an approach worth experimenting with, given that it can achieve major improvements in impact from modest changes to channels, language, techniques and terminology; the examples above show what can be possible.

Other foundational approaches that have already been outlined can be directly linked to this, such as the *Compliance Covenant* – essentially a pragmatic agreement between the company, the compliance team and employees why compliance is important, and what is required. Thereafter, developing messaging so that it includes benchmarking statements – such as '93% of the company have already completed their training' – but also using direct numeric comparisons wherever possible can be very powerful.

Also using plain English (www.plainenglish.co.uk) and similar tools to achieve easy-to-understand, direct and straightforward communications can be crucial; their simplicity will make them both inclusive and stand out. Additionally, it is important to take every opportunity to use alternative channels and direct messaging, which can prove very successful.

Moving into nudging will involve experimentation. As we have seen, minor terminology changes can make a huge difference and can sometimes bring surprising benefits; crucially, however, those communications benefits come at zero cost, and often hinge on just simple re-phrasing. Why not use *nudge* to *budge* your compliance programme?

Many companies face a formidable logistical challenge regarding compliance training for those employees who are perhaps on the road or in warehouses, and do not have straightforward access to work-based email or a PC; a mobile/cell phone may have a role, but it is arguably not ideal. Clearly, taking groups of these employees or contractors off production, distribution or customer service can also have very direct and immediate effects on performance.

As a consequence, we implemented a process nudge by creating telephone training, where employees undertake their basic training using just a phone and can do so in downtime or, indeed, from home. This was one of our most successful programmes, not least of all because – unexpectedly – by allowing the training to be undertaken at home it created an environment of trust, and greater engagement. It also represented a simple but useful *micro-learning* capability, and served to break down relatively complex and unfamiliar topics into short, standalone units of training, which could be referred to as many times as necessary, essentially whenever and wherever the learner had the need, desire and opportunity.

Moreover, also take a look for *sludge*; what would bog people down and deter them? How good is the readability, language, presentation and ease of access? If it would put you off, then it will certainly put a number of other people off.

Chapter 15: *Positive* Conflicts of Interest

Whilst most companies recognise that Conflicts of Interest are a key element of their overall compliance and ethics programme, they often discover that the practicalities of managing Conflicts of Interest (CoI) day-to-day can be very challenging, often resulting in few disclosures, and disclosures that are largely inconsequential. Is that really the position, or are there disclosures of significance that are simply just not being made?

My first experience of implementing Conflicts of Interest (CoI) resulted in a tearful single mother of three angrily confronting me about whether she was going to lose her desperately needed part-time job in her local burger bar, and whether this was what I and the company really wanted to get out of a Conflicts of Interest programme.

Clearly, it was not, but it is perceptions such as this – together with the perceived employee unease that might be caused by a Conflicts of Interest programme implementation – that often makes decision-makers, compliance officers and others essentially shy away from *determined* implementation decisions where there is no mandatory or otherwise compelling requirement. They assume – perhaps because it is easier – that the risks from Conflicts of Interest (both actual and perceived) are relatively low in reality and that there are few real and positive benefits to come out of such a programme, a situation compounded by the inevitable negative perceptions of a Conflicts of Interest programme; *What's in it for me, what happens if it affects me and why should I really tell you?*

Moreover, private life privacy – the inviolability of private life, personal and family secrets – is a key legal issue in some countries, which only compounds the concerns that companies, their employees and compliance officers may have. Also, in some countries it is widely considered culturally that holding a second job is good thing – the right thing – such that there are cultural challenges regarding what elsewhere would be seen as a disclosable potential Conflict of Interest.

For me, these factors ultimately resulted in a re-think of the programme, and the versatile Conflicts of Interest risk assessment matrix – based on type and likelihood – resulted, which can be adapted to incorporate a range of specific conflicts and risk mitigations. These actions enabled a clear focus to be initially established on the highest Conflicts of Interest risks – in senior management, procurement and in-country managers, for example – before progressively extending the process further in line with the risk matrix. Analysis of likely annual 'churn' (turnover) in employees, roles, reporting arrangements and personal/professional relationships indicated that keeping the Conflicts of Interest system up to date would be challenging, particularly when the full *request-reminder-escalation-review-feedback* cycle is taken into account, but that can be appropriately addressed within an automated process such that reports at differing points are supported.

However, as we considered earlier, how far would you go? It is generally relatively straightforward, within local laws, to identify companies and external roles registered to individuals and also where their home addresses are recorded as a registered company office, and then compare that to their Conflicts of Interest disclosure, if they have made one. Clearly, the company registered at their home address may have nothing to do with them, but in my experience, such comparisons can often throw up hitherto unidentified and questionable issues.

A Conflict of Interest can be identified in a number of ways: from an annualised report request, from a change of circumstances report, an ad hoc report, a social responsibility action, a legal/professional registration requirement or from a discovery, which can sometimes be the subject of a hotline report.

In whichever way the Conflict of Interest is reported, the complexity and nature of the circumstances – amounts, durations, intentional, accidental, etc. – can result in a wide range of potential actions, from a discussion with an employee's supervisor/manager, through to dismissal and potentially perhaps on to criminal proceedings.

Low risk of major conflicts	High risk of major conflicts
Low risk of major conflicts	High risk of major conflicts

Image: Courtesy of National Audit Office (UK)

Put simply, a Conflict of Interest can occur when a possible conflict exists (or is perceived to exist) between someone's personal interests, activities or relationships and the interests of their company or organisation. The conflict can come about in a number of ways including financial conflict, non-financial conflict and role conflict; all have the potential to be a direct or indirect conflict. Examples of a conflict would include (but are not limited to) conflicting economic interests, personal relationships, professional relationships, professional activities and also positions of authority held in the public sector.

These examples show how some types of Conflicts of Interest can occur, but there are further conflict-related nuances such as what is termed the 'revolving door' – where the promise of *future* employment, consultancies and/or board memberships can skew decision-making – that continue to be problematic internationally.

Whilst people generally recognise that a Conflict of Interest is unacceptable, there can be a perception that the consequences of such a conflict are mostly financial – inside information, promotion resulting from a relationship, a contract, a job for a relative and suchlike.

However, I often talk about a hypothetical example of a loss-of-life rail disaster which, whilst driven originally by financial concerns that resulted in a Conflict of Interest, had consequences far beyond purely financial. In this case, a signal technician left a wire loose with the result that three trains collided; many people were killed and hundreds injured. The technician had undertaken the work during their thirteenth consecutive seven-day working week, but had been working for two companies, and neither company knew about each other. In my experience, this dreadful case often brings home the realities of Conflicts of Interest, and takes people for the first time from what might be seen as a 'tick-the-box' exercise to stark reality. *It wouldn't happen here* often features heavily in people's perception of Conflicts of Interest, as does a belief that any Conflicts of Interest would only involve a handful of people at senior level; this case is one of a number that powerfully conveys how mistaken those views can be, and so helps to *destroy the myths*.

Moreover, I also then talk about what I call ***positive* Conflicts of Interest**; a properly operating Conflicts of Interest process will also enable employees to report, for example, the charitable work that they complete in their private and spare time. That then enables companies to identify the range of charitable work that is being undertaken by their employees to the potential benefit of the company and everyone concerned; one company had no idea that two of its junior employees held senior voluntary roles in charities, and it was only the implementation of their Conflicts of Interest programme that brought it to light. The employees benefited, the charities benefited and the company also benefited.

Fundamentally addressing the negative, intrusive nature of a Conflicts of Interest programme can be crucial. As we have seen, *Positive* Conflicts of Interest can be *Win-Win-Win* for the company, the employees and the charities involved. It also enables positive positioning as part of an Environmental, Social and Governance (ESG) programme, and creates clear reputational and relationship opportunities. From personal experience, a not insignificant number of employees had roles related to charities, which the company knew nothing of nor had leveraged – to everyone's benefit.

Moreover, it is this type of approach that can be leveraged to mitigate some of the concerns around Conflicts of Interest programmes that unions and, particularly, works councils in Europe will raise, notably when linked to a risk matrix which identifies where potential conflict-based risks exist. A typical example is shown below:

	Board	Directors	Senior Managers	Managers	Employees	Third Parties	Special Functions (e.g. Procurement)
High Risk							
Medium Risk							
Low Risk							
No Risk							

It important to recognise that dealing with the range of compliance-type issues on a piecemeal basis with works councils is not the best way forward, and that is why developing a *Working with Works Councils*-type strategy can be crucial, and has the potential to deliver significant benefit and value; it can be used, for example, to reset the potential perception of Conflicts of Interest as *intrusion* into one of *protection*.

Clearly, employees avoid disclosing relationships and suchlike for a number of reasons; these can include *it's my business, I don't want anyone to know* and *I don't want to cause embarrassment*, right through to a genuine fear of what might happen; will they be disciplined, lose their job – or be the subject of smirks, knowing smiles, comments and suchlike? So, as a first step it is often useful, from a number of aspects, to specify what standards are expected, their rationale and that, for example, relationships between managers and their direct or indirect reports need to be disclosed if there could be a potential issue so that the situation can be assessed, and appropriate (supportive) action taken.

Given the above, and the risks that might exist as a result of non-disclosure, it's clearly important that the reasons for the disclosure request are reiterated. Given that these issues were invariably likely to recur, I took a wider and longer-term approach, which I termed *Policy-Plus*; we have a policy, but these are additional, crucial insights and advice.

I took some time to spell out in an explanatory *Policy-Plus* note why Conflicts of Interest disclosures are important to everyone, and that they would relatively rarely result in disciplinary action. In that, I made it clear that if someone was uncomfortable just making an online report then they could talk to their manager, senior manager or to HR and, if deemed necessary, we would consider sensitively making a so-called *proxy disclosure* on their behalf. This approach and explanation seemed to make a noticeable difference, and related questions and disclosure volumes certainly increased.

I also covered what could be termed the *hygiene factors*, such that all the regular concerns – data protection, access to data and data retention for example –

were addressed. Crucially, the wide-ranging examples that were included – where undisclosed Conflicts of Interest resulted in significant fraud, financial and other consequences – proved to be powerful persuaders and served to demonstrate our genuine and legitimate interest as a company in this type of issue.

Conflicts of Interest don't stand still and so it is crucial to have appropriate processes, controls and, ideally, automated systems in place, supported by effective communications to manage changes over time as personal and professional relationships develop and new roles are undertaken by individuals themselves, and related parties. It can be easy to assume that such change is mostly employee-driven but wider organisational change can mean differing roles, reporting lines and relationships, such that a system that can auto-request disclosures which are then updated or automatically flagged should clearance need to change can prove crucial, particularly when the likely *request-reminder-escalation-review-feedback* cycle timescale is taken into account. Depending on size of company, a paper-based (spreadsheet) Conflicts of Interest process may suffice but there is a real risk that it will fall into abeyance as roles, responsibilities and organisations are restructured.

However, a systems-based approach can support the management of disclosures on a straightforward and non-intimidating basis, which then makes it easy for employees to be both thorough and forthcoming. It significantly reduces the administrative burden of non-contentious disclosures and minimises the time and effort required of employees, which moves it away from its perception as a 'chore' and leads to more high-quality disclosures containing fuller genuine information, in a simple and easy-to-understand format. This provides key data which, crucially, can then be linked with other compliance activities such as hotline case management, policy management, training/learning management and an organisation's core HR data to create an effective real-time compliance tool with wider visibility, and the potential to provide hitherto unseen insights such that it becomes an essential tool in the corporate governance armoury.

In addition to what could be termed the routine Conflicts of Interest process phases – *request-reminder-escalation-review-feedback* – there can clearly be several other phases including identification, reporting, prevention, mitigation, discipline, disclosure and cessation which will all require effective management to the point that they do not present a problem to the company. However, when not managed properly, conflicts can quickly turn into a serious matter for all parties including, potentially, clients and customers.

Ironically, managing Conflicts of Interest effectively has never been more important; for example, as company business models increasingly demand that they hire more freelancers, those same freelancers will clearly have multiple employers – with the result that potential conflicts come to the fore, particularly around critical areas such as intellectual property.

Regardless of the legal position in individual countries, some readers may well consider some of these Conflicts of Interest techniques too intrusive, unacceptable and even, perhaps, unethical. However, in reality the default response to a Conflicts of Interest process can often be a 'nil' return – justified on the basis that *it's none of their business, it's a private matter* or *it doesn't affect my work* – and so that suggests new techniques need to at least be considered, particularly for potentially high-risk situations.

Moreover, companies already utilise a range of anti-fraud techniques; why should similar techniques not be at least considered for **Anti-Conflict**, particularly given the potential linkages between Conflicts of Interest, fraud and also corruption? However good a company's Anti-Bribery & Corruption (AB&C) programme, without a comparably effective Conflicts of Interest programme, the company will potentially be exposed.

Without question, Conflicts of Interest management is a crucial element of an overall compliance programme, and represents a key component of an effective compliance *Corporate Shield*. It is crucial that a company's Conflicts of Interest process is positioned appropriately and positively otherwise reporting levels will remain low, and will also not reflect the true risks, typically as a result of avoidance. Crucially, the reporting process has to be straightforward and non-threatening, which then makes it easy for employees to be thorough and forthcoming in their disclosures at a time when they might be nervous and wary or perhaps consider the process to be unnecessary, intrusive, time-consuming and irrelevant to them.

Chapter 16: *Engaging* Ethics

It would take moments to find examples of companies, organisation, suppliers and vendors where 'ethics' features heavily in their website, advertising, statements and straplines; after all, companies clearly want to be seen as ethical – as do compliance suppliers and vendors as they drive to sell ethics- and values-based services and capabilities.

So far, so good – but it is one thing stating that your company is ethical, but how does that objective get translated and delivered throughout your organisation? After all, if asked, the majority of people would consider themselves to be ethical, even if they couldn't immediately define what that meant in reality.

This was the challenge that was brought home to me on a wet and windy morning involving a large group where I'd gone to present on compliance and ethics. Although non-scientific, from a quick show of hands it became quickly evident that although everyone in the group considered themselves to be *ethical*, translating that into specifics and examples relating to their professional and personal lives and situations proved to be quite a challenge.

What that meant for me was that – in reality – we had to do things differently if we wanted to really get people engaged with ethics and what it meant for them, and the company.

Ethical moments Most compliance and ethics officers will have used games, competitions, quizzes and similar tools and techniques to support learning, whether it is online, in-person or some combination thereof. However, sometimes those games are simply used as 'icebreakers' at events and suchlike in order to introduce some humour, and what is often overlooked is the genuine opportunity that can be afforded by relatively simple competitions.

An incident triggered me to think about running a competition for all employees to enter – either individually or as a small team – to identify ethics-related issues and opportunities around what were called 'ethical moments'; essentially, ethical dilemmas regarding what you would do and what other examples have you encountered, professionally or personally.

The thinking was that it would be a way of getting greater, wider and deeper involvement in ethics company-wide, and potentially help to provide insights to the associated risks and challenges – and opportunities.

Ethical fade and 'bounded' ethicality There is a raft of important terminology and concepts around ethics but often people – even compliance and legal officers – don't really encounter them, or utilise them. Ethical fade relates to how people do not see the potential unethical aspects of the choices they make such that the outcome is unethical, despite their best intentions. Bounded ethicality is the concept that our ability to make ethical decisions is often affected or restricted by other factors, pressures and considerations. As an example, if a bonus was crucial to your daughter's education but payment of that bonus depended on you acting unethically, then would your ethics be bounded? Would they fade when set against your 'greater good' argument?

These terms can often be represented by the 'Ethics Triangle', where an Opportunity – the bonus in this case – brings Pressure with it, and Rationalisation is then used to justify unethical acceptance – 'I'm doing it for my daughter', 'It's only this once' and suchlike.

```
          Pressure
       /         \
      / The Ethics \
     /   Triangle   \
    /                \
   Opportunity   Rationalisation
```

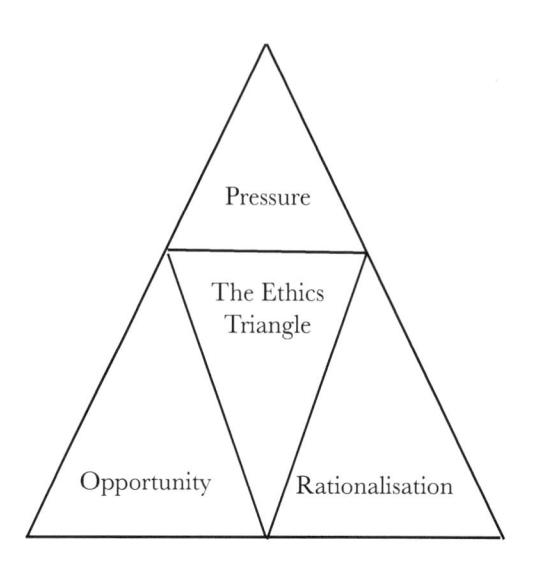

There is a raft of example dilemmas – variants of the bonus (above) where an unethical action is key to the company's success that never fail to engage. Similarly, dilemmas around ethics breaches at home and at the office, and how/why they would be dealt with differently always serve to open up ethical debate and engagement. A perennial example that similarly never fails to stimulate debate around ethics is that of the 'restaurant dilemma'. The majority of people would say that they are both honest and ethical, but would you *always* alert a server if/when you noticed you have been undercharged on your bill?

The competitions were, unquestionably, a resounding success and, amongst many other benefits that resulted, they served to really engage people and proved to be a further way of turning ethics *push* into strong employee *pull* – and the whole programme cost next to nothing. They were crucial in allowing people to hold a mirror up to themselves, and to bringing home the message that they had a personal stake in decision-making, rather than thinking – or pretending – that different rules apply at home and the office.

Embedding practical ethics and substantive ethical behaviours requires a genuine focus on ethics in order to build a sustainable and long-term ethical culture – as opposed to an ethical culture given lip service that is discarded as soon as business pressures and opportunities arise. Ethics is often well down the list – or is relegated down the list – in the issues that companies consider in sensitive decisions, yet often those decisions come back to bite them in the media and courts of public opinion. Companies committed to an ethical culture will clearly need to go well beyond the norms of periodic training and communications, and whilst there is clear overlap between compliance and ethics – such as in hotlines and Codes of Conduct – addressing issues such as job design, organisational fairness, self-interest, trust and perverse incentives offer both an opportunity and a challenge in creating an ethical company.

A useful analogy that I use is that of the *Costa Concordia*. This was a cruise ship which hit rocks in Tuscany, Italy and partially sunk, with the loss of more than 30 lives. Whilst debate has continued over the causes of the disaster and the role of the captain, there was neither the technology to warn of the impending disaster nor a preparedness to speak up and challenge. Exactly those issues – a lack of technology, analytics, insights combined with a culture of silence – can lead directly to potentially high-profile ethical failures for companies.

Chapter 17: Compliance & Ethics Competitions and Group Activities: *The Opportunity*

As we have just seen, most compliance and ethics officers will have used – or at least considered using – quizzes, games and suchlike to support learning, perhaps in conjunction with an organised 'Compliance & Ethics Week'.

Even with modest organisation, such activities can prove hugely engaging and also valuable, and can potentially help to provide insights into hitherto unseen issues – issues that we would probably never have otherwise been aware of through existing processes; the approach also serves to provide an additional feedback channel. Arguably, it is a good example of turning compliance *push* into *pull* in action.

Clearly, companies and their compliance officers continue to strive to make their compliance and ethics programmes and campaigns both interesting and memorable using a range of interactive activities such that there is genuine employee engagement, learning and long-term knowledge retention.

Whilst the gamification-type approach to compliance and ethics learning is not new, it can provide crucial support to more traditional training and learning – and a more fun, engaging aspect to the more routine and, arguably, tedious aspects of compliance, such as policy attestations and other disclosures. In this way, it can certainly engage people more deeply – but the challenge is to maintain that engagement, which can often peter out because effective and regular gamification requires effort.

What follows is a wide range of examples of compliance and ethics competitions and group activities, including a number that require relatively little organisation and preparation. All can serve to re-engage and increase awareness, and trigger new ways of thinking about compliance and ethics – whether they are used as part of an organised 'Compliance & Ethics Week' or simply as a standalone activity periodically throughout the year. However, as one small word of caution, it is important to consider how the games and competitions link to the compliance and ethics programme, company culture and employee expectations before they are launched – and it is also important that the activities are well thought through, such that they do not attract adverse feedback and, hence, disengagement.

'Your Ideas' – **Compliance and Ethics Ideas (1)** Many companies have some form of new ideas scheme for employees to submit ideas for new ways of working, products and resolutions to chronic issues, but often compliance and ethics-related entries can be very limited or, indeed, essentially zero! Probably a new idea for compliance and ethics was not something that most people wake up with!

Clearly, it was crucial to keep the competition process simple and to remove any barriers to entry, given that entries could come from a wide range of employees in a wide range of roles.

Moreover, with limited resources, the compliance and ethics team simply did not have the ability to deal with a complex entry process that would undoubtedly lead to questions, and would detract from the original simple and straightforward objective – to get people genuinely engaged both personally and professionally in the challenges and opportunities of compliance and ethics.

I didn't know what, if anything, we might receive but in the event the competition was, unquestionably, a resounding success – with extensive entries both in the individual and team categories. Some entries were more generic – for example, around compliance training – whilst some were specific, for example to what were competition law (anti-trust) practicalities. Amongst many other benefits that came from the competition, it served to really engage people, proved to be a further excellent way of turning compliance *push* into employee *pull* and provided the compliance and ethics team with a new vehicle to identify programme opportunities, issues and shortcomings.

Crucially, it also served to reinforce the message that compliance wasn't being 'done' to people, we were listening, we didn't know it all and we wanted input, regardless of role, geography, specialism and so on – and the whole ideas programme cost next to nothing, whilst garnering some extensive internal publicity that served to further reinforce the key compliance and ethics messages.

Clearly, innovative approaches to competitions, games and associated reward processes also have a role in the *pull equation* and what follows represents just some examples:

***'Show Us'* – Compliance and Ethics Ideas (2)** As a variation of the compliance and ethics ideas above, it is worth considering a photo, video or poster-based competition, which have proved to be amongst the most successful that I've run. 'Shoot C&E', 'Shoot the Issue' and 'Ethical Pride' are some examples of possible titles, which simply involves people submitting a compliance and/or ethics-related photo or video – it can be something to be commended or something to be avoided (typically, a violation) together with a caption or explanation. Team entries can be based on posters comprising photos and videos relating to a common issue, or posters can be used to provide more detailed content and information in relation to an issue.

The 'barriers to entry' are low and the resulting entries can be judged and prizes awarded. Then, they can be combined into photo or video walls or used as the basis for posters, wallpapers, backgrounds and suchlike relating to specific issues which can be produced, distributed and displayed. The competition will likely create company-wide interest, and will invariably identify a number of compliance and ethics issues and opportunities for the compliance team.

The Compliance and Ethics *Tabletop* When it comes to being well-prepared to effectively manage potential compliance issues, the tabletop exercise can be one of the single most valuable experiences for a group. From dawn raids to data breaches, tabletop exercises (or TTX as they are sometimes known) can demonstrate how a response plan would play out and where improvements should be made. A tabletop exercise brings together a group, and a facilitator presents to the team a predetermined, realistic incident scenario; participants then respond as they would in a real situation.

In what is now a well-known case, the European Commission conducted an investigation into energy companies in Germany on suspicion that anti-competitive practices were being used. Inspections were carried out at the company's Munich offices and documents were placed in a locked room overnight; the inspectors were given the supposedly only key and the room was also sealed with special stickers on which the word 'void' became visible if they were removed. However, inspectors found that the seal had been broken when they returned the next day and it later turned out that some 20 other keys to open the room were in circulation. The company was subsequently very heavily fined by the Commission for the breaking of the seal – but, ironically, it was never found to have participated in anti-competitive practices!

It is this sort of issue that tabletop exercises can highlight, including points of failure, gaps in procedures and confusion about responsibilities. For example, what would happen in your company if inspectors arrived unannounced at 6.30 am? Clearly, complexity can be added to the scenario such that it simulates a real-life incident, with new pieces of information becoming available as the exercise unfolds. A well-designed tabletop exercise will also include unexpected challenges to further test participants. For example, dawn raid response plans assume availability of all of the resources required; one such resource is people and an effective challenge could be accomplished by removing one or more of the key players.

The tabletop exercise can be a genuinely worthwhile learning experience, but will clearly require preparation, organisation and time – although once this has been invested, it can be relatively easily repeated for other audiences.

The Compliance 'Comedy Store' (1) A visit to a comedy venue in London, and experiencing the hugely engaging improv at the heart of the show, was one trigger that made me think whether this type of approach – where a competitive line of jokes is triggered in response to an issue raised by the audience – could be recreated for compliance and ethics, with a particular relevance to compliance and ethics teams.

The audience is asked for questions, issues or challenges in the compliance and ethics field. This results in a quick-fire response session from some of the assembled compliance and ethics experts, which, facilitated by the host, leads on to new issues – either triggered by the experts or sought from the audience – and so the process repeats.

Again, this exercise has the advantage that everyone is involved to the degree that they want. The session has energy and is potentially amusing, bringing 'Compliance Comedy' to the mix. It needs to be facilitated well to keep things moving and energetic. The big challenge is to avoid lengthy monotone replies from the experts, but bells can be rung or buzzers sounded to time them out, and they can then be replaced by audience members. Some audience members report that they have learnt a lot from the experience because the expert replies are more to the point and much quicker.

The Compliance 'Comedy Store' (2) – 'Reversing Roles' or 'Taking a swim in the Compliance Fish Tank'

As a further variant of the comedy venue approach, the audience vote and select hot compliance and ethics topics for discussion. The audience are divided into two groups, those *inside* the compliance fish tank and those *outside* the compliance fish tank. The group inside the compliance fish tank discuss the selected hot topic for ten minutes followed by five minutes of questions by those outside the fish tank. The groups then reverse roles and continually repeat the process until the session is completed.

The exercise has the advantage that everyone is involved, to varying degrees, in all activities. Although the preparation required and organisational difficulty is low, it will need to be facilitated well to avoid lapsing into chat; active facilitation is also again key to keeping energy and engagement levels high. One cycle, i.e. organisation, and each group taking each role just once followed by changeover will probably take approaching an hour, so it can be valuable for events.

The Corporate Shield As we have already seen, the Corporate Shield is a way of thinking about what items, activities, elements, measures, etc. go to make up the compliance and ethics shield around a company – the shield that protects it and its officers from fines, costs, reputational damage and prison, etc.

Clearly, the Corporate Shield can be completed, as normal, by delegates or small groups which then involves individual report backs and cross-comparison. However, as an alternative, it can be completed on a 'whole audience' basis where the audience is asked to shout out what items they think make up an effective Corporate Shield, and those are included in the shield template. This invariably leads to debate, and the facilitator can also inject other thoughts and items, which can often act as a key learning opportunity for members of the audience.

Once completed, delegates or the audience as a whole can be asked to rate each item for importance, and then performance in the standard way, using a scale of one to five. Those where there are the biggest numerical gaps indicate the biggest opportunities for improvement, which are then highlighted to consider what the audience could/would do to close the gap. This invariably results in extensive discussion and ideas, and recognition that compliance challenges are largely common, irrespective of geography or activity. Where there are wide variations in effectiveness ratings across the audience, this inevitably leads to impromptu discussions about how the higher ratings can be achieved – another learning opportunity.

There will also be items where the reverse is true, i.e. where they are rated of least/lowest importance, but performance or effect is highest. Those are then highlighted to the audience to consider as, essentially, it means that they/the company are very good at the things that don't matter, or matter less – and this affords the opportunity to consider and debate realigning resources to address the gaps where there are the biggest opportunities, above.

This exercise again has the advantage that most people are involved most of the time. The session has energy and, invariably, represents a genuine learning opportunity. It also requires relatively little preparation, and organisational difficulty is low.

What else? There is a raft of other compliance and ethics competitions and games that are worth considering, but they are of varying complexity and so will require varying levels of preparation and organisation; consideration also needs to be given as to whether they are to be virtual or in-person, one-off or re-used. Clearly, some may also work better if they are aimed at a single site, whereas others can be relatively readily utilised to cover multiple sites, multiple locations and even multiple countries – and, indeed, the multiple aspects may serve to increase competition and engagement.

For example, it is possible to establish a **Check Game** using a desk or even an office that is focused on compliance and ethics-related failures where delegates have to check for, find and record those issues, much along the lines of 'Escape Rooms'. Indeed, it is often possible to extend the theme further such that their findings have to be reported through existing company processes, including the hotline. This clearly has the valuable benefit of additionally familiarising delegates with aspects of compliance and ethics in a controlled environment.

A loosely compliance and ethics-based **Trivial Pursuit**-type game is another possibility which does not require too much preparation and can be updated and tailored using relevant and contemporary issues. As we have already seen, **Compliance and Ethics Dilemmas and Scenarios** can be a very useful approach, which never fail to engage and stimulate debate. Whilst compliance and ethics-related **board, card and word-search-type** games can appear to be well-received and should not be overlooked, this can be a misperception because people may be more focused on them as a competition to win a prize, rather than to increase knowledge of compliance and ethics.

Overall, whilst games and competitions have a potentially valuable role in the compliance and ethics officer's armoury, there are a number of aspects to be considered, ranging from stakeholder agreement right through to internal marketing, prizes, research, logistics and digital demands, and so early planning is invariably essential.

Chapter 18: Windscreens & Mirrors: *What gets measured gets managed*
Input, Output, Reactive, Proactive, Lagging, Leading & Insight Measures

Whilst the vast majority of compliance and ethics programmes – and compliance and ethics officers – utilise measures, or metrics, of performance, many of these measures are *input* (or activity), rather than *output*-based or proactive; essentially, they are 'looking through the mirror' (reactive) as opposed to 'looking through the windscreen/windshield' (predictive). However, there can be a perception that getting the input measures, such as training, right will result in a compliant company – with output measures deemed more challenging, such that they receive less focus. Unfortunately, despite the best training, policies and intentions, retaliation, for example, can still be prevalent, and that is why output measures in reality are crucial.

Perhaps confusingly, there is a range of measurement terms that are often used near-interchangeably – leading and lagging measures are, similarly, two types of measurements used when assessing performance. A lagging indicator would be, for example, the number of injuries on a building site. A leading safety indicator is a predictive measurement such as the percentage of people wearing hi-visibility jackets on that building site, on the basis that being more visible should reduce certain types of accident. The difference between the two is that a lagging indicator can largely only record what has happened whereas a leading indicator can influence change.

Clearly, the key issue is to measure results, but measuring activity is invariably records-based and so easier and more often reported, e.g. training completion rates, policy attestations or Conflicts of Interest responses. These are clearly important numbers, but don't truly offer insight; by comparison, scores from a training follow-up test and questionnaire will arguably go some way to demonstrate how much of the training an employee actually retained, and so do offer a degree of insight.

Put simply, an hour of training is the input, but how it succeeds in changing the employees' attitudes and behaviours is the output – but, clearly, the challenge of measuring that change is not insignificant and will take time, and require a range of contributory indicator measures. Moreover, compliance and ethics officers need output measures to help and support them in anticipating issues before they arise – but that challenge is often compounded by compliance not owning relevant data sources within a company, or not fully considering what data might be available and how it could be combined and leveraged.

For a compliance officer, these types of insight measures can potentially be crucial, particularly those utilising 'disparate data' – measures derived from disparate sources of data that could offer crucial insights into their compliance and ethics programme and its performance.

However, thought is often not really given to these disparate sources of data and bringing them together because the opportunity is not immediately apparent and so what they could offer together is missed. There can also be a tendency – particularly in larger companies – to look at data vertically rather than laterally, e.g. division, department or team data rather than necessarily comparative data across disparate teams, where normalisation may be just one of the challenges. Failure to utilise the data in this way can often expose companies to risk, such as bribery and corruption; customer travel and hospitality, for example, might be fully authorised within a division, but without a lateral view and the necessary reconciliations, the overall level of company hospitality expenditure on a client, customer or government may not necessarily be joined up – and it is this overall position that regulators and investigations will invariably focus on.

As an example, a company authorised through an individual's management chain the gift of a bottle of Scotch to a government minister. Although the individual was a government minister and hence higher risk, it was considered that the gift of a single bottle of Scotch was acceptable. At face value, the authorisation process had worked as required.

However, this was a large company and the authorisation process did not have the necessary infrastructure to consider other bottles of Scotch and gifts that might be given to that same government minister and their department.

It took a review to show that the level of hospitality and gift-giving to the minister was clearly excessive, and could have represented a significant bribery risk. Everything had been properly authorised vertically – but without any real lateral consideration.

Similarly, in a review undertaken on behalf of one company, it was discovered that over a near three-year period, one department reportedly accepted hospitality 718 times, which equates to circa five times per week. However, over the same period another comparably-sized department only reported accepting hospitality 20 times. Whilst there may be some variation in activities, the inescapable conclusion was that that latter department had significantly and consistently under-reported hospitality. Clearly, questions remain as to the reasons why that level of under-reporting had been maintained, and allowed, over such a relatively long period.

In what is a good example of where the data exists but is not being utilised in novel ways, as we have previously seen, an analysis of lunchtime and late afternoon supplier/vendor visits to the main sourcing/procurement offices derived from the visitor and door entry logs was undertaken – on the basis that given the timings there was a high likelihood that a meal of some type would be involved, and potentially other gift-giving. The analysis only served to reveal a pattern of significant under-reporting of hospitality which, whilst the data integrity was not perfect, provided some valuable insights and analytics, and formed the basis for other similar approaches. However, its success in conveying the message that declaring Gifts & Hospitality/Gifts, Travel & Entertainment was important proved to be invaluable, and arguably achieved more sustained improvement than endless reminders.

Moreover, as we have also previously seen, hotline report data and HR-type data on pay, bonuses, promotions, overtime, shift allocations and suchlike clearly already exists – but are, arguably, 'siloed' such that they are not brought together in a way that could then be used to analyse and identify possible retaliation incidents, risks and patterns.

Clearly, it may not be possible to establish measures for all hitherto-unmeasured aspects of a compliance and ethics programme, but many can be measured – if not directly, then indirectly or by inference sufficient for a compliance officer's purposes. The focus on data by regulators should also never be underestimated, and some will often expect compliance officers to be able to quickly list the measures they use, and the data that they monitor. It is also crucial to consider, measure and address the issues that can cause *disengagement* with compliance and ethics. For example, measure what is termed the Compliance and Ethics *Engagement Gap* if you are able. People that meet their compliance and ethics training deadlines, always read compliance and ethics communications and take a reasonable time for both are not only engaged employees, but also important assets. How could they be utilised – and, also, is there any analysis and action that could be undertaken in relation to people who *don't* display this same level of commitment? As an extension of this, what analysis could be undertaken to indicate any senior managers (and perhaps others) who are potentially using their assistants to complete their training, such as consecutive completion of assistant and manager training.

As we have considered earlier, genuinely *proactive* testing and measurement of compliance and ethics is still relatively limited, but test reports to hotlines, mystery shopping, training phishing, 'pulse' surveys and mock (staged) dawn raids are all examples of where such an approach can prove both very valuable and eye-opening.

Whilst, as we have seen, most companies use measures to support their compliance and ethics programme and to make decisions, they also often rely on what I would term the *usual suspects*; for example, hotline reports, training completion rates, policy attestations, Conflicts of Interest responses and suchlike. Whilst these are clearly without question essential, what companies often do not do is really examine what would deliver genuine insight, and what data there is that could be utilised to deliver that objective.

Clearly, there is also the potential for 'pulse' and other surveys, and the opportunity to utilise proactive compliance testing on higher-risk aspects of compliance and ethics that might otherwise remain unassessed. In addition, the *Cost of Compliance* can be a powerful measure in assessing and positioning a programme, and has the potential to be developed into a broader Return on Investment (ROI) measure.

Although it can often be overlooked, exception data can also be crucial, such as focusing on the 3% of people who did *not* complete their training rather than solely on congratulations for the 97% who did. As we have seen from the *Engagement Gap* above, if it is available then using data related to training – for example, how long someone took to read a compliance and ethics communication, how long it took them to complete their training, when it was done, where they encountered issues, what their test results were and also whether, potentially, someone completed it for them – can be very insightful.

Similarly, data relating to remedial actions, disciplinary processes and outcomes is clearly crucial to a well-managed compliance and ethics programme. However, looking for anomalies – such as geographic and other variations in outcomes from disciplinary cases, for example what is termed the *Gender Punishment Gap* – can again be revealing, and such anomalies will certainly need to be addressed.

Whilst many companies will have an established (perhaps annualised) formal risk register process, tools such as the *Corporate Shield* can provide more immediate, straightforward, granular and insightful assessments to support compliance and ethics teams and their company's unique risk profile. Whatever is used, a risk-based assessment framework is crucial to establishing Key Risk Indicators (KRIs) and the measures needed to identify and underpin programme improvements. Normalising these metrics on a per-employee basis can often have a powerful effect on their perception, relevance and use.

As we have considered, there is often data available but it is not used, or not used to its full potential. For example, it is one thing using metrics to simply *look through the mirror* – incidents of harassment, for example, in Europe in the last quarter. But, why not mine that data more for lessons to learn and to *look through the windscreen/windshield* – proactive and predictive, rather than reactive; for example, analysis showing that a harassment report made in Europe at a particular location has an 80% probability of resulting in retaliation can then be utilised to support reporters, implement training, maintain vigilance and initiate change. Also, *join all the dots*; investigation reports, audit reports, security reports and hotline data, for example, can all enable issues to be homed in on, but are often not brought together in this way because the data sources are disparate, and don't immediately lend themselves to assimilation because of timings, formats, availability and other factors. Failure to bring the data together in this way means that compliance issues are often not anticipated – and perhaps only become visible once they have reached problematic dimensions. The issues with this entirely reactive approach are clearly manifold; the company is inevitably in a poor position to anticipate and react and, overall, there is little evidence of an effective compliance programme of the type necessary to satisfy regulators and to keep the company out of the courts.

Culture is always crucial to a compliance and ethics programme, but is invariably the most difficult aspect to measure, as evidenced by the rarity of compliance and ethics events that do not include culture in their content.

However, by bringing together a broad mix of measures that could be deemed *culture indicators* – such as employee surveys, relevant hotline reports and also retaliation incidents – it is possible to establish some reasonably sound measure of culture. Surveys and questionnaires are not necessarily a true indication of a company's culture given that employee self-reports of this nature are often unreliable, but they do have a role.

Crucially, however, it is important not to *fall into the traps*, i.e. failings in organisational justice, failings in the hotline reporting process such as lack of follow-up, report conclusion, differential treatment based on seniority and similar issues will near-guarantee a poor culture of compliance and ethics, and poor reputations. Moreover, raising a compliance issue that then doesn't get addressed, or addressed satisfactorily, will only result in that person or team not raising an issue again – and bad news travels fast.

Overall, measures are clearly crucial to all compliance and ethics programmes, not only in terms of implementing and operating the programme, identifying shortcomings and opportunities and deciding on strategy, but also in terms of demonstrating performance of the programme, whether that is internally to senior management or the board, or externally to critics, customers and regulators.

Chapter 19: *Working with Works Councils* in Europe

There is no question that works councils in Europe can exert a powerful and effective influence. Works councils provide representation for employees in the workplace in some – but not all – European Union (EU) Member States (countries); some Member States recognise unions, and some potentially recognise both works councils and unions.

Whilst their influence varies across the EU, in countries such as Germany, works councils have a long-established history and extensive participation rights enshrined in legislation. Their powers include rights to information and consultation and extend to an effective right of veto on some issues as a result of what is termed 'co-determination'; essentially a 'seat at the table' such that they have decision-making rights along with senior teams, which can be comprehensive, depending on the nature of the issue, although it invariably includes Codes of Conduct, technical equipment, software and associated training.

It is for this reason that for companies operating in the EU, implementation of sensitive compliance-type activities – for example hotlines and Conflicts of Interest disclosures – will inevitably involve works councils, a situation that can often be disconcerting to compliance officers who may have had little previous experience in this regard.

European works councils are, as their name implies, bodies that represent the European employees of a company. Through a works council, employees are informed and consulted by management on the performance of the business and on key issues and decisions that could, for example, affect their future employment, working conditions or contractual terms at a European level. The works council can also raise and negotiate issues of concern to them, and to company employees. It should be stressed from the outset that although there are linkages – usually through common elected representatives – works councils are not trade unions; the main function of the works council is participation in management decision-making; for trade unions it is largely collective bargaining. This distinction is, clearly, crucial.

Works councils in Europe have a fairly substantial history and have become an established part of industrial relations infrastructure. However, whilst works councils have expanded their coverage in Europe in recent years – largely through support from European Union legislation – there is wide diversity in the structure and operation of works councils across the EU Member States.

The challenge in international companies is to ensure that appropriate consultation takes place with works councils in a structured, agreed and timely way. This can be particularly demanding where, for example, a global programme is being introduced that requires multinational works council consultation by compliance officers and managers who are largely unfamiliar with these bodies – and, indeed, do not consider the potential industry, national and international collaboration that takes place across works councils. The European Union Directive relating to works councils applies to all European Union Member States (27) plus the three other countries of the European Economic Area (EEA – Iceland, Liechtenstein and Norway).

It should be stressed that not all companies operating in Europe will have works councils; there are a number of associated threshold tests regarding their establishment, and this is a further reason why compliance officers will often not have encountered works councils previously, and do not necessarily have experience of working with them – although they may have comparable experience with unions and similar bodies. Moreover, individual Member States are able to enact their own statutes that engender, or otherwise, the establishment of works councils, with a variety of resulting legislation and approaches.

The three European countries where works councils are at their strongest are arguably Germany, Austria and the Netherlands – where works councils represent a traditional and fundamental institution of employee cooperation. In these countries, works councils are empowered with significant rights to co-determination, which is a form of joint decision-making where the works council has to give its consent before certain types of management decision can be taken and implemented.

Briefing and working with works councils, internationally, on the types of programmes that many compliance and ethics officers will be involved with can be challenging. As an example, one international household-name company had a major programme delayed for over a year because of issues with their works councils – and it should be noted that works councils legislation is not without 'teeth'; typically, this might include criminal offences and penalties, damages for lack of consultation and also, potentially, the works council could request a court order barring management from implementing a project if, for example, the council has not been properly informed and consulted.

Given this background, it is essential that compliance officers involved in implementing what could be deemed 'sensitive' programmes – such as hotlines and Conflicts of Interest – first identify if there is a works council or councils in the countries of operation/implementation. It is also helpful at this stage to identify further information about the nature of the works council, including local sensitivities, which may be historic.

Although perhaps *unconventional*, rather than minimising and delaying contact with the works council, it can often be beneficial for everyone involved to proactively map out the compliance and ethics programme at the outset. Crucially, it can also be invaluable to position the sometimes unstated benefits of hotlines, Conflicts of Interest disclosures, policy attestations and other elements of the programme for works councils; for example, to take the perception that Conflicts of Interest disclosures could be intrusive and position the *positive* and protection benefits, for both the company and its employees – a vital objective largely shared with the works council.

This approach can help build commitment and co-cooperation, and facilitate 'high-trust, low conflict relations' between works councils and the compliance and ethics team.

The Appendices include an indication – and provides a simple checklist – of the key issues that are central to effective relationships with works councils. Additionally, there is a basic *Works Councils: Typical Questions & Answers* document which has proved helpful in the implementation of a hotline and associated Case Manager systems; it can be readily adapted for Conflicts of Interest and other system and process implementations.

Chapter 20: *Active* Anti-Bribery & Corruption:
Is It Reasonable, Could I Reciprocate?

Anti-Bribery & Corruption (AB&C) often features high on many compliance officer's priorities, and invariably the foundations are around policies, training, education and communications.

Clearly, it is crucial that companies have the right AB&C policies in place and, in many cases, companies will ask that their people have attested to them; this includes 'linked' policies such as Gifts & Hospitality/Gifts, Travel & Entertainment – activities which can directly provide a vehicle for bribery and corruption, both *inbound* and *outbound*.

It is essential that the policies reflect local laws, requirements and standards; for example, in one bribery case a company made cash *per diem* payments to delegates from a Central African country. That was arguably bad enough, but those payments of between $120 and $200 *per diem* were made at a time when the country's gross *annual* per capita income was just $710 – ultimately leading to the company being fined heavily for 'elaborate, circuitous schemes' of bribery.

'Tone at the Top' and corporate culture are also clearly key elements of bribery prevention and it is essential that due diligence on third parties is carried out regularly, reliably and without fear or favour.

However, a key element of establishing an effective AB&C programme is to implement meaningful and relevant training, recognising that many people taking the training will question their presence, and its relevance to them; after all, *I'd never take a bribe*.

It could be argued that, perhaps, *outbound* bribery (e.g. gifts and hospitality given) is more straightforward to police in that the giver (your employee) can refer to policies and processes before doing so, and such payments will need to be sourced; as a consequence, although they may be (well) disguised, they may be able to be reconciled with expense payments to some degree.

However, *inbound* bribery (e.g. gifts and hospitality received) can be more difficult to police, for a host of reasons. Sometimes, for example, the *bite to eat* after work can become a lavish, five-star restaurant meal, perhaps even involving an expensive gift. This is an example of the 'sliding scale of bribery' that we consider in this chapter, where the acceptable meal turns into unacceptable bribery – often unexpectedly, leaving the receiver unsure of what to do. This can particularly be the case where *perverse incentives* are at play, where a good relationship with a supplier or vendor is crucial to a project being delivered, and also crucial to the employee in terms of their bonus, career prospects and suchlike.

Gifts and Hospitality/Gifts, Travel and Entertainment policies are clearly essential, but they can become unwieldy and hence a *shelf policy* – unused and not referred to – particularly when, for example, the detailed complexities of multiple geographies are involved, with their individual financial limits and other requirements. It is for this reason that most global and multinational companies either take the decision to adopt a universal standard policy or attempt to rationalise their policy by utilising country groupings supported by exception statements.

In my experience, one hugely valuable approach can be to establish simple gifts and hospitality tests, and then turn those into easily remembered phrases to give a *rule-of-thumb*. One example is that of *Is it Reasonable, Could I Reciprocate?*; would the hospitality being offered be deemed reasonable in the court of public, colleague or family opinion, and would I be able to provide the same level of hospitality if the roles were reversed? It is only a rule of thumb, but having that firmly in people's minds can act as a good check-and-balance that can be applied mentally immediately.

For this reason, it can be crucial to use images to open up engaging debate on bribery rather than it being perceived as *just more training*. Moreover, there are plenty of case examples of where an individual attended the training and 'ticked the box' in doing so, but paid scant attention, learnt little and subsequently ended-up in trouble.

The *Bribery and Corruption Triangle* is a good example and encapsulates the three factors that drive virtually all types of bribery – an opportunity that either presents itself or is sought out, financial or other pressures to take the bribe and then rationalisation; *it's only this once, I'm doing it for my family* and similar justifications.

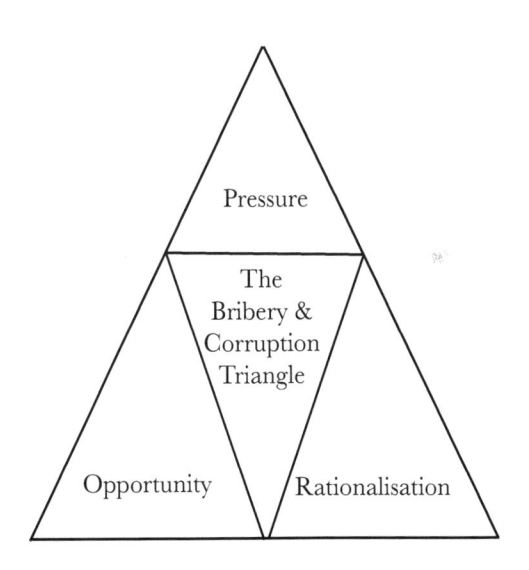

```
            /\
           /  \
          / Pressure \
         /------------\
        /  The         \
       / Bribery &      \
      / Corruption       \
     /  Triangle          \
    /----------------------\
   / Opportunity | Rationalisation \
  /_____\
```

A technique known as *Stand in the Space* is an extension of this in that by visualising standing in the space – for example, the 'space' between the company and its suppliers/vendors – companies can consider, and discuss, how bribery might be perpetrated.

The triangle enables a company to, firstly, consider the bribery *supply side*, i.e. where would monies, goods and services for bribery come from within a company; these sources would clearly include expenses, petty cash, company gifts and hospitality, bank accounts, company cards and other payment sources. Stories abound of compressor invoices being, in reality, disguised payments for cars destined to be used as bribes. In some renowned bribery cases, at the heart of the issue was a large number of hitherto unknown company bank accounts that were being utilised to funnel bribery funds.

On the *demand side*, where could, and would, demands for bribery come from; governments, overseas operations and major customers are all potentially principal areas of risk where a company needs to be certain that it has the controls, processes and analytics in place.

Finally, the *bribery environment* covers the environment both inside and outside a company. Internally, has the objective or target-setting process created an environment that employees might resort to bribes in order to meet their targets, for example, often known (as we have seen) as 'perverse incentives'. Externally, is bribery considered the 'norm' in a particular industry, sector or geography and, if so, could regulatory reporting and other approaches be utilised to address it?

The *Sliding Scale of Bribery* is also a very useful visual challenge tool when educating employees about bribery; for example, what starts out as a straightforward hospitality lunch with a supplier develops into a visit to their overseas production plant, a lavish dinner, generous gifts, out-of-hours socialising with their team, staying on for a few days for sightseeing and then involving your family. At what point does a business relationship based on trust slide into a business relationship based on bribery? Again, it may be easy to say this doesn't happen, but it does and can easily catch out the unwary.
What would be the environmental factors to create that slide – and what would the factors be to prevent it? As an example, where a contract is minor to a company but major to a supplier or vendor, the environment for what is termed *Differential Bribery* can be created; the contract may be

managed by a junior employee in the company, but a senior employee in the supplier/vendor. These types of scenarios, made specific to a company or industry, can present a vivid image of the *tipping point* into bribery.

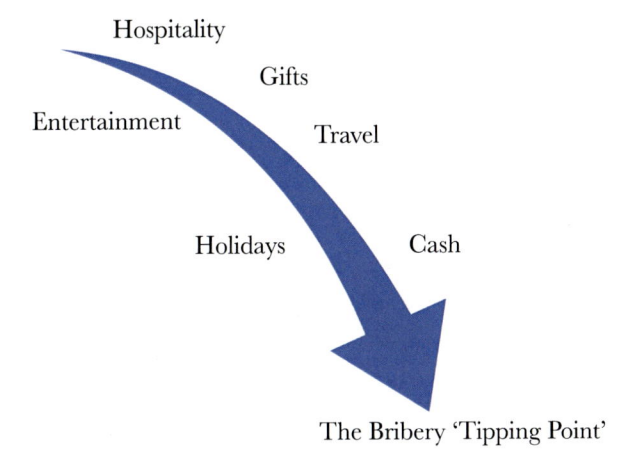

Hospitality
Gifts
Entertainment
Travel
Holidays
Cash

The Bribery 'Tipping Point'

Finally, the ABC of fraud is frequently applied in the field of law enforcement but is equally applicable to bribery and corruption. Whilst it might be deemed 'negative', it can represent a very useful and visually appealing approach to consider in relation to bribery and corruption prevention.

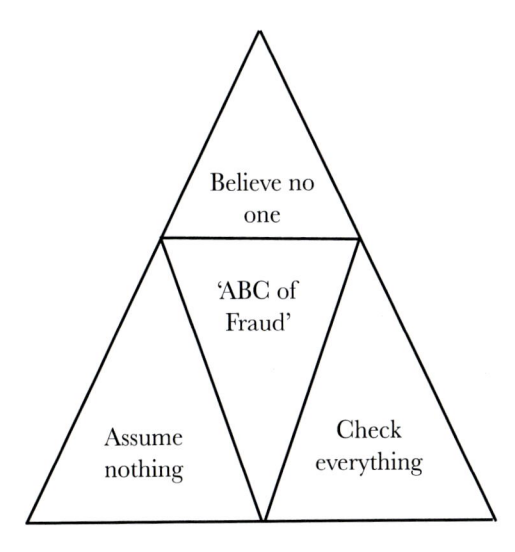

- Believe no one
- 'ABC of Fraud'
- Assume nothing
- Check everything

There are other tools that can be utilised in the detection of bribery – in all its facets – and although most compliance offers will not deploy them themselves, it can nonetheless be crucial that compliance officers are aware of them in working with finance, security investigations and other teams.

A good example is that of Benford's Law. Intuitively, if you were to take a group of naturally occurring numbers starting with 1, 2, 3, etc. (ignoring any leading zeros) it would be reasonable to think that there would be roughly the *same* number of numbers that begin with each different digit, i.e. the proportion of numbers beginning with each different digit would be roughly 1/9th or 11.1%. However, in many cases that is wrong and, surprisingly, for many types of numerical data, the distribution of first digits is highly skewed, with 1 being the most common digit and 9 the least common.

There is a precise mathematical relationship behind this phenomenon – a logarithmic relationship – which is known as Benford's Law, or the first-digit law.

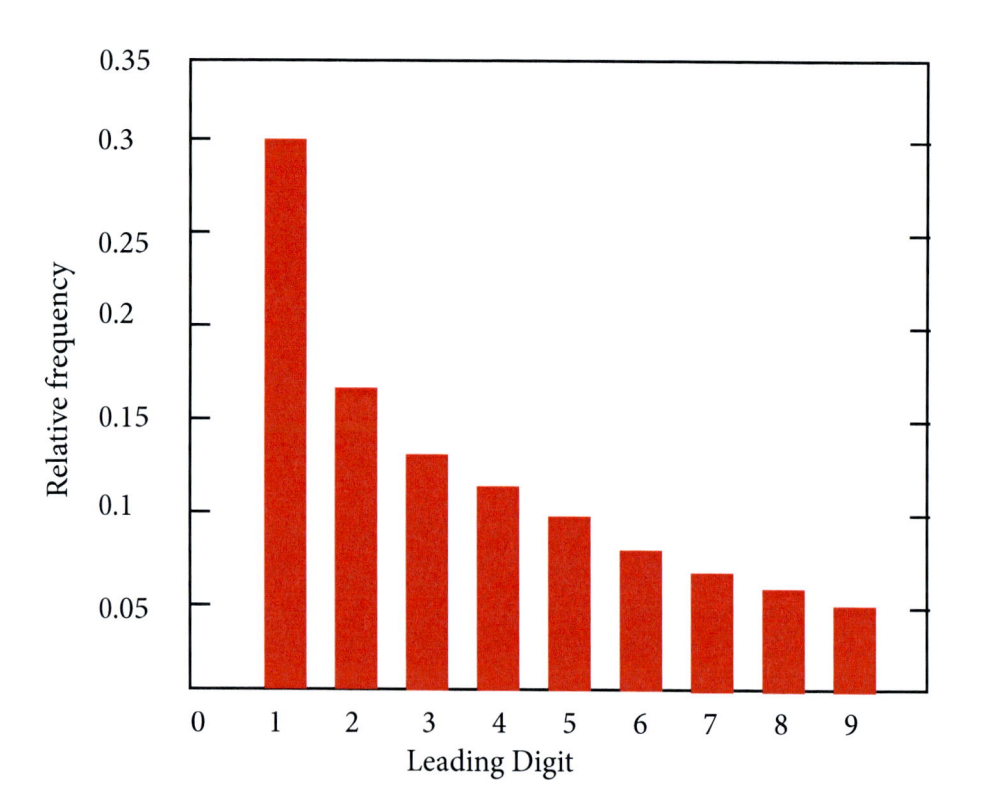

Benford's Law states that in lists of numbers from many real-life sources of data, the leading digit is distributed in a specific and non-uniform way. According to this law, the first digit is 1 about 30% of the time, 2 about 18% and larger digits occur as the leading digit with lower and lower frequency, to the point where 9 as a first digit occurs less than 5% of the time.

Whilst Benford's Law gives an interesting and surprising result, it has direct relevance to the work of compliance officers in the areas of bribery, corruption and fraud.

One good example is that if someone attempts to falsify invoices or accounts then, inevitably, they will have to invent some data. When trying to do this, the tendency is for people to use too many numbers starting with digits in the mid-range such as 5, 6 or 7 – and not enough numbers starting with 1. Clearly, this violation of Benford's Law would immediately set alarm bells ringing.

In procurement and compliance, Benford's Law can be used to show any skew in values, such as invoices; typically, this analysis would highlight invoices concentrated around, for example, 4 – to get below a signing threshold of £500 or £5,000. If suppliers are attempting to circumvent such rules, usually with collusion – tacit or otherwise – then what else is going on? Similarly, such creativity might be being used to create an illicit 'bribery fund'.

Chapter 21: Compliance, Ethics – and *Practical* Persuasion

Clearly, persuasion – in all its facets – is a key element of any compliance or ethics officer's role; it could be argued that a *persuasive* compliance officer will be an effective compliance officer. Not surprisingly, therefore, there is a raft of excellent articles and books relating to the theory of persuasion, and what are the generally recognised five *Principles of Persuasion*. There are links to some of those excellent pieces at the end of this book, but the purpose here is certainly not to duplicate those; it is about considering how some of the tools, techniques and approaches that we have considered earlier can be powerfully and, most importantly, *practically* persuasive.

Reciprocation This principle broadly relates to the area of *what's in it for me?* that we have considered earlier – and given that this is a key principle, it's not surprising that many compliance officers struggle to become genuinely influential. Put simply, if you give a positive experience to people then they will generally want to give something in return. But all that *pushing* means that the relationship between compliance and the organisation is arguably one-sided; after all, many people see anything compliance-related largely as an imposition such that compliance and ethics get pushed down the priorities, delayed and deferred. Changing the relationship in practice requires focus, but can deliver substantial benefits. For example, why not radically change the online or paper-based compliance training record – either way, it's rarely seen or referred to – into a compliance *passport* with value and status to the individual; make compliance of value, and reciprocity will follow.

Liking Right or wrong, compliance and compliance officers can sometimes be portrayed as the classic distant and out-of-touch headquarters function.

In reality, people are more likely to engage with compliance if they have a basic understanding of the issues, and know, respect and like the people involved. So get out there; get out from behind the paperwork, bring the message with you and become the genuine face of compliance. From personal experience, a talk to a hundred field engineers about ethics, and what it really meant for them personally and professionally in their role was a crucial turning point for me, and something that would never, ever have been achieved with an email barrage from behind a desk.

Commitment and consistency There is plenty of research that shows that people generally like to finish what they start. As we've seen, a *Compliance Covenant*-type statement and agreement that unequivocally lays out the grounds as to why compliance and ethics are so important can be a crucial foundation for change. It can be the trigger for people to get on and complete their training, not on a piecemeal basis but as part of a programme that is perceived as integral to a company's well-being, good governance and overall *Corporate Shield*. Getting that initial messaging right at the outset and focusing effort on getting people started showed, without question, that the approach was far more effective than endless email chases and escalations later.

As an extension of this, it can be that compliance programmes obey a *saw-tooth* pattern; commitment, investment and interest is low and the programme sits at the bottom of the hypothetical saw-tooth until the time comes that there is an issue or investigation – affecting the company or industry – that demands investment of significant monies and resources, and time from the board. The programme then moves up the saw-tooth until the point that the problem recedes, whereupon the compliance programme focus is allowed to *decay* back down the saw-tooth, at least until the next time – hence the saw-tooth pattern. This *yawing* approach can convey a raft of wrong messages, and is another reason why establishing and delivering ongoing commitment and consistency is crucially important.

Scarcity I learned the hard way just how essential it is to tailor training to specific audiences, rather than take a 'one-size-fits-all' approach. However, a compliance programme ostensibly aimed at, say, directors and vice-presidents but extended to other groups can send a powerful message of both exclusivity and inclusivity, as does a special programme tailored for people managers, for example; a programme 'reserved' in this way will get far more traction than something generic pushed out to every employee, regardless of responsibilities. Provided that the ethical aspects are respected, then this useful, but arguably unconventional and underused, approach can offer wider benefits for compliance and ethics officers.

Authority and social proof When people are uncertain about a course of action, they tend to look to those around them to guide their decisions and actions; we have previously seen this in how powerful the *other people do* nudge in relation to taking litter home became. People will take their lead from those that they respect as authorities and experts, such as shop-floor leaders; they will also want to know what everyone else is doing – especially their peers; as a consequence, social proof is a powerful tool for driving compliance and ethics programmes, and training. However, it is also essential to deal with both motivating *and* de-motivating influences; for example, I discovered that about 300 employees in one very large company had rarely, if ever, completed their compliance training and had managed to hide largely undisturbed below the 95% completion headlines. Although they only represented some 0.3% of the overall workforce, the thought of those 300 was anathema to me; dealing with the issue sent a swift and powerful *we are serious* compliance message to the organisation.

The *Principles of Persuasion* and their respective practical examples, above, show just some of the areas that compliance officers can, and should, focus on if they are to genuinely persuade, influence and impact, both personally and professionally.

However, there are other approaches and qualities that will help turn a corporate compliance officer into an *influential* compliance officer. Well-constructed ethical dilemmas, for example, can split audiences, trigger debate and serve to wake people up from the apathy of *it wouldn't happen here* to the real challenges of compliance and ethics.

There can also be many *myths of compliance*, even in the eyes of the board and senior managers, and destroying those myths can fundamentally reset perceptions, and the consequent ability to influence. For example, compliance can be perceived as an expensive overhead but re-calculating the cost of compliance on a per-employee basis can present a totally different picture of good value-for-money. From personal experience, companies that I have worked with would manage their programmes such that the level of compliance and ethics investment spend was around £10 to £22 ($12 to $27) per employee per annum, which seems pretty good value. By comparison, as we have seen, fines can represent some 150 times that figure – and to put £10 to £22 in perspective, it equates to just a couple of trips on the Underground (subway) in London. Supporting data and simple analytics such as this can represent a powerful tool in the compliance officer's armoury as they build their reputation, and sphere of respect and influence.

Although easy to discount, the personal and professional qualities required in a persuasive and influential compliance officer should never be ignored; amongst others, these clearly include determination, persistence, assertiveness, focus and intuition – coupled, at times, with a robust approach and thick skin!

We have previously seen typical examples of the perennial, common or core challenges faced by compliance officers where, in order to address them, persuasion will invariably be a central requirement.

They include:

i. Implementing, establishing and operating effective training, education, communications, whistleblowing and disclosures (e.g. Conflicts of Interest and Gifts, Travel & Entertainment (GT&E)/ Gifts & Hospitality (G&H))
ii. Getting engagement and commitment from employees, contractors and those in other work-based relationships, and also addressing indifference
iii. Managing compliance and ethics in what can be a four- or five-generation workplace
iv. Responding to change in compliance and ethics, including legislation, regulation, technology and societal, such as social media and social responsibility
v. Managing compliance and ethics internationally, including legislative developments and differences
vi. Addressing the challenge of third parties and Third-Part Risk Management (TPRM)
vii. Understanding and addressing compliance and ethics risk
viii. Getting support from senior/top management
ix. Managing internal and external relationships, including key stakeholders and regulatory-type bodies
x. Making best use of available resources

As we have considered, employees, contractors, third parties and others will clearly not necessarily commit or 'buy-in' to compliance and ethics, and there will be a significant spread of engagement across a company, including a number who will often see it as a 'chore', and consign it to something that is put off for as long as possible, and then done as quickly as possible. Clearly, it is essential that the compliance officers are able to *sell* and position compliance and ethics to all stakeholders, and whilst training can often be at the heart of achieving this objective and getting the cultural message across, it has to be both effective and engaging, otherwise it will only succeed in *disengaging* – and will certainly not be the catalyst for culture and behaviour change, which can be a long road if the norm has historically been indifference.

A key step in obtaining support from senior management and the board is to address the issues and perceptions that can make them see compliance and ethics largely as a business intrusive cost, with little genuine added-value. In one company, I became so agitated by the lack of engagement by the board that I put them on the spot to tell me individually how much they each thought the company spent on compliance per employee, on the basis that cost in this case seemed to be a major preoccupation. The outcome was that some of those figures were more than *ten times* the actual, which served to fundamentally shift their perspective once they were aware of the realities of the compliance and ethics *value equation*. When normalised against fines that similar companies had received – not to mention all the associated costs, adverse publicity and reputational damage – it became a powerful and long-term message that served to facilitate deeper and more meaningful understanding of the risks, and the value provided by the team in dealing with what were potentially serious issues.

Appendix 1: The Corporate Shield: Assessing your Programmes

As we have considered earlier, what keeps a company compliant and ethical? What are the activities, processes, controls and systems that make up a company's compliance and ethics programme, and do they join up? How would a compliance officer know, and how could they be evaluated?

Moreover, what in simple terms protects that company; what does the company have in place that shields them from compliance failure, and the fines, reputational damage and other consequences that come from such a failure. It was a simple concept, and one that everyone pretty quickly understood and the reasoning behind it. From that came the Corporate Shield – a simple pictorial and practical representation of a company's compliance and ethics programme, which can be used to identify the compliance processes, controls and systems that are in place, together with the gaps.

The Corporate Shield can be used by individuals, small groups and teams and also provides the facility for a quantitative analysis of an overall compliance and ethics programme, and its individual elements – which invariably delivers very surprising results, as we will see in a moment. I have used it internationally with a range of audiences at a variety of events and it is always well-received, and proves to be an eye-opener for delegates. Crucially, it can be completed quickly in less than 30 minutes end-to-end or slowly where the desire is to facilitate greater debate around the analysis.

The simple Corporate Shield template is shown on the next page.

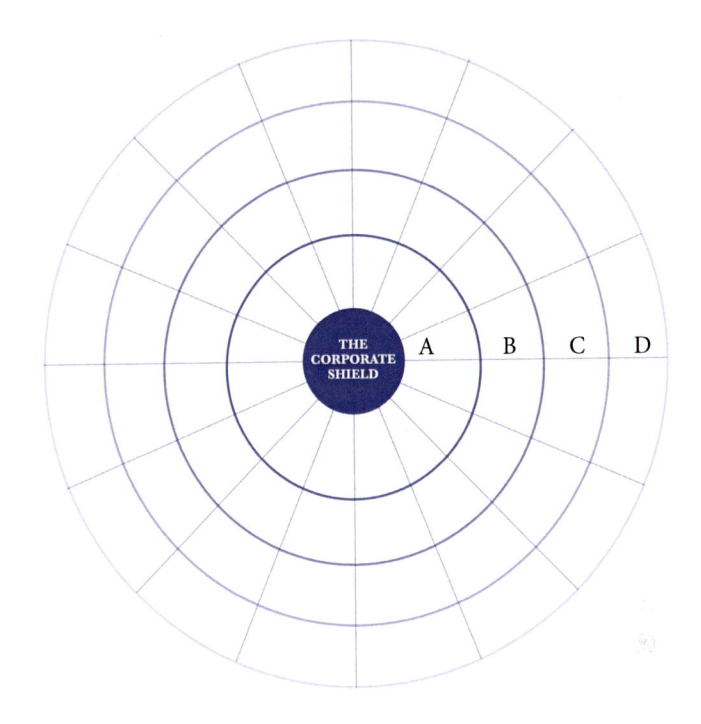

Step 1: There are 16 boxes in the outer circle 'D', which are used to identify the elements, activities, processes, systems and suchlike of a compliance and ethics programme that shield and protect the company, organisation, division, subsidiary, etc. Examples of those elements, activities, processes, etc. would potentially include training, communications, whistleblowing, codes, policies, disclosures and audit together with processes regarding competition law (anti-trust), Anti-Bribery & Corruption (AB&C), data privacy, anti-retaliation, etc.

What shields your company? Some typical examples
• Training
• Phishing exercises
• Communications programme
• Automated compliance controls/alerts
• Whistleblowing
• Third-Party Risk Management (TPRM)
• EU Whistleblower Protection Directive

• Risk Assessment
• Anti-Retaliation policy and process
• Mock Dawn Raids and other compliance exercises
• Codes of Conduct
• Conflict of Interest policy and disclosure process
• Anti-Bribery & Corruption policy and process
• Data protection policy and process
• Disclosures/Disclosure Processes
• Published reports – internally & externally
• Auditing/Internal Audit (including unannounced audits)
• Analytics – programme
• External Audit
• Relationship management – regulatory bodies et al
• 'Tone at the Top'
• Compliance Ambassador Programme
• Monitoring regulatory/legislative/compliance developments
• Board Briefing Programme
• Compliance home working strategy
• Works Councils programme

I almost always see all 16 boxes completed and quite often delegates, colleagues, etc. will list more on another sheet. Moreover, regardless of whether the Corporate Shield is completed by individuals, small groups or teams, it will lead to debate, which only serves to support engagement, learning, review and comparisons.

Step 2: Circle 'C' is then used to rate each of the entries in circle 'D' in terms of Importance to the company and to its compliance programme, using a 1 to 5 scale where 5 is highly important and 1 is low importance.

Step 3: Similarly, circle 'B' is then used to rate each of the entries in circle 'D' in terms of Performance, using again a 1 to 5 scale where 5 is high performance and 1 is low performance.

As an example, whistleblowing could be deemed highly important to a company and so would warrant a '5' rating in 'C' – but the company's performance in relation to whistleblowing could be considered low/poor and so this would result in '1' rating in 'B'. Clearly, a similar rating would also result if, for example, the company had no whistleblowing process in place. This rating process will again lead to debate and engagement.

Step 4:
Finally, circle 'A' is then used to calculate the results – the gaps (differences) between the Importance and Performance ratings in 'C' and 'B' for each element. Using the example above, a '5' rating in 'C' and a '1' rating in 'B' would result in a '4' rating in 'A', i.e. the result of C minus B; any minus signs should be retained.

The results can then readily be easily and quickly reviewed and, undoubtedly, this process will again lead to debate and engagement.

Any positive 'A' markings will either be 4, 3, 2, 1 or 0. Clearly, the primary focus should be on the 4s and 3s which indicate the gaps that need to be closed, and represent the greatest opportunity, because these activities, programmes, systems and capabilities are of greatest importance, but low performance.

Any negative 'A' markings mean that the company is performing activities well that don't matter, or matter less than others. Congratulations – but clearly, this is a waste of effort, and that effort could be redirected to other more important activities, including those identified immediately above. It should be noted that this analysis usually comes as a shock, and invariably results in further debate and soul-searching.

As a further stage, it is possible to ascertain from the group's shields those elements and activities that were most frequently identified. Again, whistleblowing might be an example, and the spread of markings and the reasons behind that spread offers a key opportunity for debate and learning. There will almost certainly be significant variations in how people perceive a particular risk, and understanding the reasons behind that can be both revealing and invaluable.

Additionally, the Shield can also be developed to take a Russian Doll approach, and provide a drill-down or more granular view of a specific element of the shield. For example, if whistleblowing is a key element of the overall shield, then the shield approach can be similarly applied specifically to whistleblowing, and all the contributory elements, activities, processes and systems of that – for example, telephony, intake, case management, anti-retaliation, reporter feedback and communications. Clearly, there a host of such elements and multiple stakeholders, and the Shield offers the opportunity to exhaustively identify and evaluate them on an end-to-end basis.

In summary:

- What **elements and activities** make up your Compliance and Ethics programme? (circle 'D')
- Rate the **Importance** of each one (1 to 5, where '5' is High) (circle 'C')
- Rate the **Performance** of each one (1 to 5, where '5' is High) (circle 'B')
- For each element and activity, **subtract** the Performance rating from the Importance rating
- **Biggest numerical 'gaps'** (4, 3 or 2) in scores show primary areas for improvement
- **Negative gaps** show high performance in areas of less importance, i.e. you are very good at things that don't matter, or matter less

An example of a completed Corporate Shield is shown overleaf, identifying 16 activities which make up a typical Compliance and Ethics programme. The activities identified are (i) whistleblowing, (ii) training, (iii) comms (communications), (iv) audit, (v) anti-retaliation, (vi) mock dawn raids, (vii) analytics, (viii) CoI (Conflicts of Interest), (ix) AB&C (Anti-Bribery & Corruption), (x) TPRM (Third-Party Risk Management), (xi) reporting, (xii) Codes of Conduct, (xiii) EU Whistleblower Protection Directive, (xiv) country legislation (monitoring), (xv) regulatory changes (monitoring) and (xvi) risk assessment. The ratings and analyses show that:

- the biggest numerical gaps are anti-retaliation at 4 and Conflict of Interest at 3, which are consequently the primary areas for improvement
- the biggest negative gaps, i.e. high performance in areas of less importance are audit at -3 and mock dawn raids, country legislation (monitoring) and regulatory changes (monitoring) all at -2. These offer the opportunity to redirect effort to other more important activities, including those identified immediately above

Whilst the Corporate Shield is a simple pictorial and practical representation of a company's compliance and ethics programme, a comparison between the compliance and ethics issues identified in the Shield and also a company's risk register can prove to be invaluable and, sometimes, an alert to hitherto unaddressed risks.

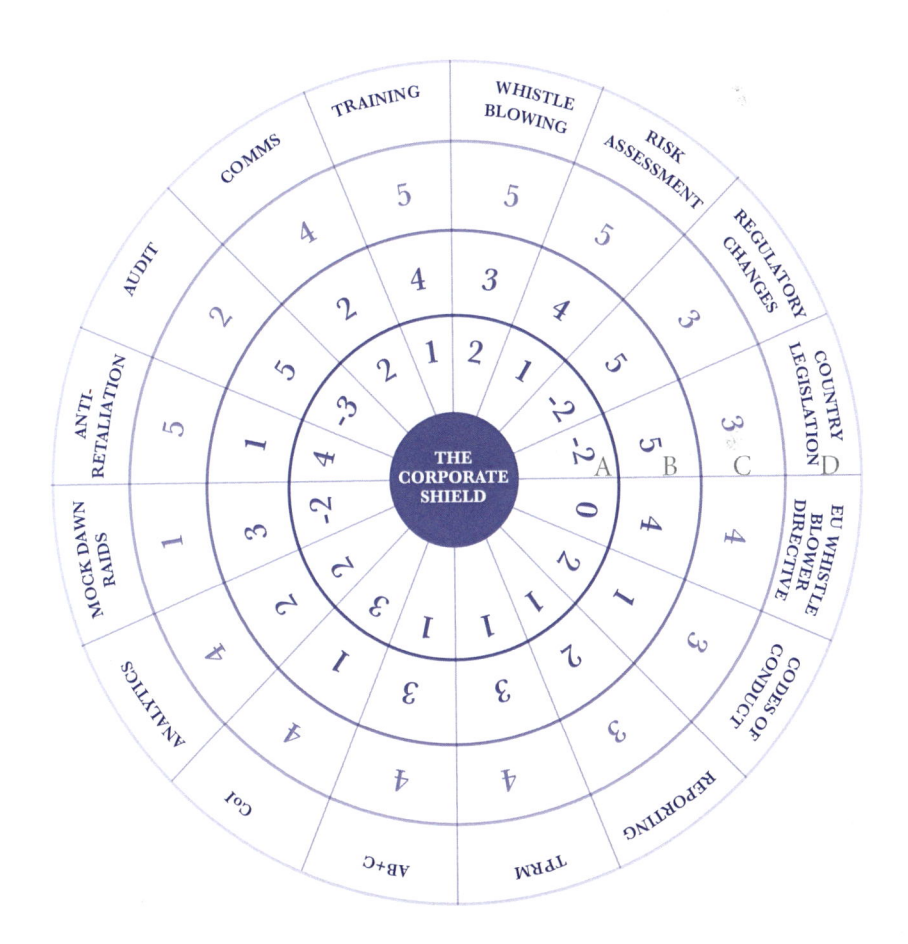

Appendix 2: The Corporate Shield: Further Typical Compliance & Ethics Actions

- Compliance and Ethics training – general
- Compliance and Ethics training – role-specific
- Policies
- Processes
- Separation of duties
- Internal audit (including unannounced audits)
- External audit
- Anti-Bribery & Corruption training/policy/process
- Segregation of duties
- Whistleblowing hotline/helpline and associated policy & process
- Whistleblowing anti-retaliation
- Whistleblowing branding
- EU Whistleblower Protection Directive
- Phishing exercises
- Compliance and ethics testing programmes e.g. whistleblowing
- Financial regulations – policy, process, training
- Data compliance/security, cyber-security, firewalls etc.
- Data protection/GDPR etc.
- Communications – briefings, awareness, consequences etc.
- Benford's Law-type anomaly analysis
- Code of Conduct/Ethics
- Conflicts of Interest policy and process
- Third-party compliance policy and process
- Effective due diligence processes for suppliers and contractors
- Understanding of 'international dimensions' of compliance and ethics
- Works councils

- Compliance and ethics metrics and measures – insight data
- Gifts & Hospitality/Gifts, Travel and Entertainment
- Effective & consistent supervisory processes (especially where the small size of an organisation makes segregation of duties difficult and/or where employees are working remotely/in isolation)
- HR team relationships, including data, policy and process
- Legal team relationships
- Security team relationships
- Investigations
- Competition/Anti-Trust – policy, process, training
- Mock dawn raids

Appendix 3: Anti-Retaliation Checklist
(Including EU Whistleblower Protection Directive requirements)

Anti-retaliation policy & documentation		
Does your organisation have an anti-retaliation policy, endorsed by top management?	• Yes • No • Some/Part • Don't Know/Not Sure • Not Applicable/None	Comments
Does your organisation's Code of Conduct include the anti-retaliation policy, or an anti-retaliation section?	• Yes • No • Some/Part • Don't Know/Not Sure • Not Applicable/None	Comments
Do your organisation's employee handbooks, vendor/supplier documents, onboarding briefings and suchlike address retaliation?	• Yes • No • Some/Part • Don't Know/Not Sure • Not Applicable/None	Comments
Is your organisation's anti-retaliation policy or Code of Conduct (if includes anti-retaliation) published externally (e.g. outside the firewall)?	• Yes • No • Some/Part • Don't Know/Not Sure • Not Applicable/None	Comments
Anti-retaliation communications		
Does your organisation communicate the anti-retaliation policy and message to all employees?	• Yes • No • Some/Part • Don't Know/Not Sure • Not Applicable/None	Comments

Does your organisation communicate the anti-retaliation policy and message to everyone with whom it has a 'work-based relationship'? This includes (but is not limited to) temporary workers, fixed-term contract workers, freelancers, contractors, trainees, interns (paid or unpaid) and volunteers.	• Yes • No • Some/Part • Don't Know/Not Sure • Not Applicable/None	Comments
Does your organisation communicate the anti-retaliation policy and message to all vendors, suppliers and other third parties covered by the EU Whistleblower Protection Directive? (See Section 6, below.)	• Yes • No • Some/Part • Don't Know/Not Sure • Not Applicable/None	Comments

Anti-retaliation training & understanding

Does your organisation train managers and supervisors on anti-retaliation, including identification and prevention?	• Yes • No • Some/Part • Don't Know/Not Sure • Not Applicable/None	Comments
Does your organisation cascade the anti-retaliation (in full or in part) to employees, contractors and others?	• Yes • No • Some/Part • Don't Know/Not Sure • Not Applicable/None	Comments
Is your organisation satisfied that your workforce – managers, supervisors, employees, contractors and others – understands the various forms of retaliation, and how it can take place (e.g. supervisory retaliation, peer retaliation, overt ('hard') retaliation, subtle ('soft') retaliation, deferred retaliation)	• Yes • No • Some/Part • Don't Know/Not Sure • Not Applicable/None	Comments
Is retaliation addressed as part of your organisation's onboarding processes?	• Yes • No • Some/Part • Don't Know/Not Sure • Not Applicable/None	Comments

Anti-retaliation & whistleblowing/hotline reporting		
Is retaliation in its various forms and how it can take place addressed within your organisation's whistleblowing/hotline reporting processes?	• Yes • No • Some/Part • Don't Know/Not Sure • Not Applicable/None	Comments
Research has shown that 6% to 10% of retaliation takes place more than six months after a whistleblowing/hotline report is made, so reporter support is not a 'once-and-done' activity. Do your organisation's follow-up processes, practices, record-keeping and training address this type of longer-term retaliation risk?	• Yes • No • Some/Part • Don't Know/Not Sure • Not Applicable/None	Comments
Does your organisation have designated and impartial person(s) and/or teams in place and trained to case manage retaliation reports to conclusion and also to maintain communications with the involved parties?	• Yes • No • Some/Part • Don't Know/Not Sure • Not Applicable/None	Comments
External reporting of retaliation		
Retaliation can take place externally to an organisation. This can often take the form of a vendor/supplier losing their contract, having their order levels cut and suchlike although some external retaliation can be far more extreme. Does your organisation have the necessary processes, channels and training in place to address external reporting of retaliation, which is invariably more challenging than internal reporting?	• Yes • No • Some/Part • Don't Know/Not Sure • Not Applicable/None	Comments
Anti-retaliation analytics		
Does your organisation utilise any type of retaliation analytics to identify potential incidents of retaliation, even where they have not been reported (this may be a result of fear, for example)?	• Yes • No • Some/Part • Don't Know/Not Sure • Not Applicable/None	Comments

Anti-retaliation & practices enshrined in the EU Whistleblower Protection Directive			
Would your organisation's policies, processes and record-keeping be sufficient in practice to discharge the Reverse burden of proof regarding retaliation enshrined in the Whistleblower Protection Directive? *(This requires the organisation to be able to prove that it did not retaliate against individual(s); the individual(s) no longer have to prove that they were retaliated against.)*	• Yes • No • Some/Part • Don't Know/Not Sure • Not Applicable/None	Comments	
The Whistleblower Protection Directive extends retaliation protection (notably) to third parties or facilitators – such as colleagues or relatives – who could be affected by a hotline report or other disclosure. Protections also apply to those whose work-based relationship has yet to begin, such as through pre-contractual negotiations, or where it has ended. Does your organisation have the necessary processes, channels and training in place to address these types of external retaliation reports under the Whistleblower Protection Directive?	• Yes • No • Some/Part • Don't Know/Not Sure • Not Applicable/None	Comment	
Will your organisation's policies, processes and record-keeping ensure compliance with the relevant action/response/conclusion timeframes specified in the Whistleblower Protection Directive?	• Yes • No • Some/Part • Don't Know/Not Sure • Not Applicable/None	Comment	

Appendix 4: Working with Works Councils – Checklist

This is a typical checklist intended to cover a common works council scenario; that of a new activity, programme, training, etc. being introduced as part of a wider activity in a multinational company.

The checklist is aimed at those who have limited experience of works councils which, as a result of limited exposure, is very often the case.

Clearly, not all questions in the checklist will be relevant to all companies – nor will they be relevant to all activities; however, they will provide a useful template that can be adapted to a wide variety of circumstances.

Working with Works Councils – Checklist
Section 1: Relevance to Works Councils

Q1. Does your activity, programme, training, roll-out, project, etc. fall under the general remit of works councils, i.e. is it relevant? Does it need you to deal with works council(s)?

Q2. If the answer to Q1 is NO, then is there good reason for involving works council(s), e.g. for awareness, good industrial relations, etc.?

Q3. Does the activity, programme, training, etc. fall under the remit of all works councils, irrespective of geography?

Q4. If the answer to Q3 is NO, then which works councils are affected?

Section 2: Strategy for Works Councils

Q5. What is the end objective of involving works council(s) – both now and in the future?

Q6. Is the objective in Q5 directly related to this activity, programme, training, etc. or is it part of a wider/longer-term strategy?

Q7. What are the channel(s) to the works council? Is there a single channel, route or interface to all works council(s) in the organisation?

Q8. Who in your organisation is responsible for the interface with works councils, or is it undertaken on a per project/occasion basis?

Q9. What is the preferred method of communication – correspondence, presentation or conference call?

Q10. Will the strategy necessitate communication with individual works council(s), or could/should the communication be generic to all affected works councils?

Q11. Do the company's works councils work closely together – and should this be a factor when considering the overall strategy for works councils?

Q12. What issues are sensitive and/or crucial and how will they be handled?

Q13. What decisions and/or input are required from the works council(s)?

Q14. What benefits – of all kinds – will there be for employees and the works council(s) from these decisions and/or inputs?

Q15. What considerations (if any) need to be given to related trade union activities and/or issues?

Section 3: Logistics for Works Councils

Q16. What would be the ideal timing for communication with the works council(s)? How would that be best achieved? How does this dovetail with the works council(s) schedule?

Q17. What material will be provided to/left with the works council(s)? What will be the purpose?

Q18. Is there a 'standard communications route' for works council(s), e.g. provision of papers to scheduled meetings, and would that be the appropriate channel in this case?

Q19. Is there a preferred presentational approach, such as an in-country manager?

Q20. Are there other works council issues that are relevant to this activity, programme, training, etc. that needs to be factored in? Does the works council have any other 'hot issues/concerns'?

Q21. Who will attend the works council session? Who do they represent? What is their background, and likely issues/concerns?

Section 4: Post Works Council

Q22. Were the works council objective(s) achieved? If not, why not – and what is the plan to recover the situation?

Q23. What actions were agreed with the works council – and what is the plan to discharge them in a timely way?

Q24. What lessons can be learnt from this interaction with the works council?

Q25. What will be the works council strategy going forward? Would it, for example, be beneficial for a regular 'update' session to be held with (selected) works council(s), recognising that some works councils have better/more active attendees than others?

Appendix 5: Implementing XYZ Co's new Hotline & Case Manager System
Works Councils: Typical Questions & Answers

Preamble

Whilst we believe that XYZ Co is a well-managed, caring and supportive company, in any company of our size from time-to-time issues may arise that cannot be reported and/or resolved locally through normal channels, i.e. through an immediate supervisor or manager, or HR. Clearly, implementing an effective Hotline & Case Manager system to address those issues is considered best practice, and is essential for any company of our size and global footprint.

However, whilst we have historically always had a Hotline capability within our company, it became evident that the current system had several shortcomings with the consequence that, for example, the level of reports was relatively low, and the case management process left opportunities for improvement. It is for these and other reasons that we decided to implement a new Hotline & Case Manager system, and selected the ABC Company ('ABC') as our partner.

These Works Councils Questions & Answers are intended to help you in local communications about the implementation of our new Hotline & Case Manager system. Please feel free to add to them, and we would certainly welcome feedback on the questions that have been raised in your own discussions.

Section 1: Introduction to the new Hotline & Case Manager System

Q1.1: What is a Hotline & Case Manager System?
A1.1: *A Hotline is often known as a Whistleblower Hotline, Hotline, speak-up line or something similar. Whatever it's called, it fulfils broadly the same function – to enable employees and sometimes others to raise issues (and questions) confidentially and, in those countries where it is allowed, anonymously.*

Although the term 'Hotline' implies that a telephone line is used to make reports, with the new system that is just one of the possible channels through which reports can be made.

If the Hotline is the front end of the system, then Case Manager is the back end; as its name implies, it is the database that is used to support the resolution of reports process, whatever that resolution might eventually be.

Q1.2: Why does XYZ Co need a Hotline & Case Manager System?

A1.2: *Whilst we believe that XYZ Co is a well-managed, caring and supportive company, in any company of our size from time-to-time issues may arise that cannot be reported and/or resolved locally through normal channels i.e. through an immediate supervisor or manager, or HR.*

It is here that the Hotline comes in to enable employees and sometimes others to raise issues (and questions) confidentially and, in those countries where it is allowed, anonymously. The Case Manager is then used to support the resolution of reports process, whatever that resolution might eventually be

Implementing an effective Hotline & Case Manager system is considered best practice, and is essential for any company of our size and global footprint.

Q1.3 Are there examples of why XYZ Co might need a Hotline & Case Manager System?

A1.3 *Yes. Ikea, Siemens and Tesco (a major UK retailer) have all experienced situations where it has only been a whistleblower contacting their Hotline that revealed issues of bribery and false accounting.*

These examples show that implementing an effective Hotline & Case Manager system is considered best practice, and is essential for any company of our size and global footprint; indeed, in many countries, legislation demands it.

Q1.4: If this is new, did we have something else before?

A1.4: *Yes, we did have – and still do have – a Hotline capability which will remain operational until the new one is launched. However, whilst it was fit-for-purpose originally, Hotlines and case management have moved on significantly, and the new Hotline represents the 'state-of-the-art'.*

The level of reports that we received through the current Hotline was relatively low, and the case management process left opportunities for improvement. It is for these and other reasons that we decided to implement a new Hotline & Case Manager system, and selected the ABC Company (below) as our partner.

Q1.5: How did we choose the ABC Company?

A1.5: The ABC Company is a leading company specialising in ethics and compliance-related systems and software; many of the ABC Company's customers are major household names. The company has grown fast and this reflects how many companies are moving to the ABC Company because of the capabilities that they offer. Details of the ABC Company can be found online.

They were chosen after an extensive tender process where, on an objective and numeric evaluation basis, they came out best for XYZ Co's needs.

Section 2: Processes

Q2.1: How does the new Hotline & Case Manager System work? What about anonymity?

A2.1: Reports can be made in several ways, including phone and online. The Hotline operates 24/7/365 so wherever someone is, they will be able to make a report at a time that suits them, in their own language. If the report is made by phone, then it will be free of charge to the caller.

A report to the Hotline can be made easily, either using a structured approach, i.e. by choosing the most relevant scenario and issue(s) or by a summarised approach, i.e. a spoken or written summary.

The Hotline enables employees and others to raise issues (and questions) confidentially and, in those countries where it is allowed, anonymously. If someone chooses to be anonymous, then they can be partially anonymous (anonymous to XYZ Co but known to the ABC Company) or fully anonymous to everyone. Whilst the decision on this is clearly up to the individual and will depend on circumstances, the advantage of giving some contact details is that, if necessary, further information can be obtained from the reporter as the issue is investigated.

Guidance, regulations and laws regarding hotlines and anonymity vary around the world, sometimes because of historical reasons, but the vast majority of countries now allow reports to be made anonymously.

Once a report has been made, then Case Manager enables the report to be directed to the correct person or people for investigation, subject to a series of clever 'auto-escalation' rules within the ABC Company system that will prevent, for example, a complaint about an individual being investigated by that same individual.

Case Manager also provides the necessary processes and controls to ensure that the case is managed and progressed to timely resolution. Clearly, further input from and/or feedback to the reporter will often be required and Case Manager provides the ability to add that information. The overall objective is that cases will be managed effectively with feedback to the reporter at all stages.

There will be a target resolution time recognising that cases can vary widely in their complexity.

Q2.2: What are the data flows relating to the system?
A2.2: *Overall, these are as outlined in A2.1, above.*

Q2.3: How long is the report data retained?
A2.3: *Report data will be retained in line with the laws and regulations of XYZ Co's countries of operation, which do vary.*

Q2.4: What's the difference between a Hotline and a Helpline?
A2.4: *Unlike some others, the ABC Company system has the ability to deal with both Hotline reports and questions, and not just Hotline-type incident reports. Sometimes, reporters contacting the Hotline will actually just want a question answered rather than to make report – and also reporters contacting the Hotline with a question may then decide to make a report; this is one benefit of an integrated Hotline and Helpline.*

Q2.5: If we didn't receive many reports before, why will we have more now?
A2.5: *We should receive more reports for several reasons; for example, the new system will offer more reporting channels and will be more user-friendly. There will also be a sustained communications campaign about the new system.*

Q2.6:   When is the 'go live' date for the new system?

A2.6:   *The system will be rolled-out progressively during 20XX. Details for each of XYZ Co's countries of operation will be communicated as soon as they have been confirmed.*

Section 3: Compliance

Q3.1:   What about international Data Privacy, and the General Data Protection Regulation (GDPR)?

A3.1:   *The system will be implemented to fully meet international data privacy rules, regulations and laws. Clearly, these can vary considerably – particularly in relation to Hotlines and whistleblowing – and so it is a significant challenge to meet this objective, but the implementation is being fully supported by our in-country legal teams and data privacy experts.*

The General Data Protection Regulation (GDPR) is a regulation by which the European Commission strengthened data protection across what are now the 27 Member States (countries) of the European Union (EU). One of the primary objectives of the GDPR was to simplify the regulatory environment for international business by unifying regulation across the EU. The GDPR originally came into effect on 25 May 2018 and XYZ Co – and the Hotline & Case Manager system – are GDPR-compliant.

Q3.2:   What about Information Security (InfoSec) and the new System?

A3.2:   *Information security, sometimes shortened to InfoSec, is the practice of preventing unauthorised access, use, disclosure, disruption, modification, inspection, recording or destruction of information regardless of whether the data is electronic or physical.*

Clearly, given the potential nature of the Hotline & Case Manager system data, information security is crucial and has been extensively tested and independently assessed.

Q3.3:   How do Hotline reporters know that their personal data is safe?

A3.3:   *The range of measures taken by the ABC Company ensures that the company meets and exceed data privacy requirements.*

The ABC Company also adheres to the strictest security protocols which are independently audited annually.

XYZ Co has appropriate company data privacy processes in place to ensure that Hotline reports are protected and compliant.

Q3.4: What about the new EU legislation – the 'Whistleblower Protection Directive'?

A3.4: *In 2019, the European Parliament published their new directive on the 'protection of persons who report breaches of Union law' - now referred to as the 'Whistleblower Protection Directive'. Under the Directive, companies with more than 250 widely-defined workers were required to comply with the legislation by 17 December 2021, and those with between 50 and 249 by 17 December 2023.*

The new legislation is a directive; a directive specifies legislative results that must be achieved by each EU Member State (country), but they are free to decide how to transpose the directive into national laws, so there are legislative variations and differences across the EU.

The ABC Company's Hotlines & Case Manager system has extensive compliance capabilities and XYZ Co will be compliant with the legislation in each Member State where it operates.

Section 4: Other

Q4.1: Don't whistleblowers often face retaliation?

A4.1: *It is true that some whistleblowers can face various forms of retaliation – but XYZ Co has a clear anti-retaliation policy and any proven incidents of retaliation will be treated with the utmost seriousness, up to and including dismissal/termination. This is a key requirement under the EU Whistleblower Protection Directive outlined in A3.4, above.*

Q4.2: What does the new Hotline & Case Manager system mean for employees and others?

A4.2: *Implementing the new Hotline & Case Manager system sends a clear message to XYZ Co employees and others that the company is serious about listening to their issues and concerns and ensuring that they are resolved quickly and effectively, as part of a wider focus on good management and treating people fairly. For the first time, the new system* means that we are 'taking the Hotline to our employees' and giving them and others the opportunity to report what they want, where they want and when they want.

Q4.3: What does the new Hotline & Case Manager system mean for supervisors and managers?

A4.3: *In addition to what it means for employees, above, supervisors and managers will also be able to make reports on behalf of colleagues, for example, who report to them, or raise issues with them.*

Q4.4: What does the new Hotline & Case Manager system mean for works councils?

A4.4 *In any company of our size, from time-to-time issues may arise that cannot be reported and/or resolved locally through normal channels, i.e. through an immediate supervisor or manager, or HR.*

It is here that the Hotline comes in to enable employees (and sometimes others) to raise issues (and questions) confidentially and, in those countries where it is allowed, anonymously. As a consequence, the Hotline & Case Manager means better corporate governance, employee support and transparency which helps everyone, including works councils, in resolving issues and improving the working environment at XYZ Co.

The Hotline & Case Manager also provides extensive data analytics which can provide the data necessary to identify trends, issues and other developments to the benefit of everyone at XYZ Co.

The ABC Company Hotline has been implemented very successfully internationally, including EU Member States (countries) where works councils operate.

Q4.5: What does the new Hotline & Case Manager system mean for our third parties?

A4.5: *Third parties – such as our vendors and suppliers – will also be potentially able to access the new Hotline & Case Manager system. Clearly, XYZ Co has a large number of vendors, suppliers and others that are crucial to our company, and opening the Hotline & Case Manager system to them sends a clear message that XYZ Co is serious about listening in the event that they have any issues or concerns. This is also a specific requirement under the EU Whistleblower Protection Directive outlined in A3.4, above.*

Q4.6: How will the new Hotline & Case Manager system be publicised?

A4.6: *There will be an extensive awareness programme including both direct and indirect communications, such as posters. There will be a focus on ensuring that colleagues are made aware of the Hotline number for their country, and where they can find further information should they need it – such as the Hotline URL (web address) – bearing in mind that for privacy reasons people may decide to make reports away from work. Again, ensuring awareness of the system is a key requirement under the EU Whistleblower Protection Directive outlined in A3.4, above.*

Section 5: Contacts

Q5.1: Who are our contacts regarding the new Hotline & Case Manager system?

A5.1: *There will be a range of local, regional and central contacts. Details will be published as we get nearer the go-live date.*

Appendix 6: Conflicts of Interest (CoI) – Programme Performance and Risk Assessment Questionnaire

This provides a questionnaire which is intended to enable companies to produce a thorough Conflicts of Interest 'state of readiness' assessment, or at least act as a reminder of potential programme roll-out issues and considerations. It takes a broad approach to elements that can factor into the success – or otherwise – of a Conflicts of Interest programme, such as Tone-at-the-Top, policies, training and communications.

A Conflict of Interest can be identified in a number of ways: from an annualised report, from a change of circumstances report, an ad hoc report, a social responsibility action, a legal/professional registration requirement or from a discovery, which can sometimes be the subject of a Whistleblower Hotline report.

In whichever way the Conflict of Interest is reported, the complexity and nature of the circumstances – amounts, durations, intentional, accidental, etc. – can result in a wide range of potential actions, from a discussion with an employee's supervisor/manager, through to dismissal and on to criminal proceedings.

CoI Programme Area	CoI Programme Element	CoI Programme: Status and Readiness Red/ Amber/ Green
A	**Overall**	
1. Current CoI programme	a. Does your organisation currently have some form of CoI programme in place?	
	b. How would you broadly rate the overall effectiveness of that programme now?	
2. Current compliance capability	a. How would you broadly rate your organisation's current compliance performance?	
	b. How would you broadly rate your organisation's current compliance culture?	
	c. An effective CoI programme will require employees to disclose personal information and information not directly related to their jobs (such as names and roles of relatives in roles where there could be a conflict). Does your organisation have the culture of employee transparency necessary to support full and frank disclosure?	
	d. Are there any areas in your organisation that potentially present a high CoI risk (such as procurement) where the compliance culture would not necessarily support an effective CoI programme?	
	e. Are there any areas in your organisation that potentially present a high CoI risk (such as procurement) where the compliance culture would not necessarily support an effective CoI programme?	
B	**Governance and Organisation**	
1 Tone-at-the-Top	a. Would you say that the board (or equivalent) does/will provide significant support to the CoI programme on a proactive basis?	
	b. Would you say that the board or leadership team does not provide significant/proactive support on CoI – but will deal with issues more on a reactive basis, as and when they arise?	

		c. Would you say that the organisation's knowledge of, and focus on, CoI is variable and depends on the understanding and commitment of individual leaders?			
		d. Would you say that there is currently little or no knowledge, focus and commitment to CoI?			
		e. Will this be a first CoI programme or a programme re-launch for the organisation?			
	CoI management structure	a. Has management responsibility for CoI (including implementation) been agreed? Failing that, will it be agreed in time for roll-out?			
		b. Have CoI resources (both internal and external) been agreed?			
C		Policies and Procedures			
	1. Scope of policy	a. Does/will the CoI programme require all employees in the organisation to make a disclosure?			
		b. Does/will the CoI programme require the board and all senior managers to make a disclosure?			
		c. Does/will the CoI programme require all managers to make a disclosure?			
		d. Does/will the CoI programme require all employees in high-risk areas (such as procurement) to make a disclosure?			
	2. Disclosure policy	a. For those employees required to make a disclosure, will the disclosure cover personal information, such as outside roles (both with and without compensation)?			
		a. For those employees required to make a declaration, will the disclosure extend to requiring employees to disclose information not directly related to their jobs (such as names and roles of relatives in roles where there could be a conflict)?			
	3. Policy communication	a. Does/will every employee in the organisation receive a copy of the policy or be prompted to access it?			
		b. Does/will every employee affected by the policy either receive a copy of the policy or be prompted to access it?			

4. Training, education and awareness	a. Will every employee in the organisation receive training in CoI?	
	b. Will every employee affected by the policy receive training in CoI?	
	c. Will every employee involved in managing and supporting the policy (such as HR) receive training in CoI?	
	d. Will there be other CoI education and awareness activities, such as targeted poster campaigns?	
5. Communications and strategy	a. Was there/will there be a CoI kick-off plan, including communications?	
	b. How frequently is it planned that CoI compliance obligations will be communicated to the target audience(s)? NOTE: Monthly = High, Six-monthly = Medium, Annually = Low)	
	c. Is there a Whistleblower Hotline that can be used for CoI issues?	
	d. Does the Whistleblower Hotline support anonymous reporting of CoI issues?	
	e. Is there a helpline that can be used for CoI-related questions?	
6. Assessment and escalation	a. Has/will the CoI management assessment and escalation protocol been implemented (i.e. in the event of a Conflict of Interest what is the process)?	
	b. Has/will the CoI enforcement process been implemented (i.e. in the event of a Conflict of Interest what will be the remediation steps, timescales and integration with disciplinary actions)?	
7. Periodic reassessment and certification	a. What is/will be the frequency of the CoI programme review? NOTE: Annually = High, two-yearly = Medium, three-yearly = Low)	
	b. What is/will be the frequency that employees will need to update their personal CoI disclosures? NOTE: Annually = High, two-yearly = Medium, three-yearly = Low)	
8. Verification of disclosures	a. Employee disclosures are/will be verified NOTE: High-risk employees only = High, some employees only = Medium, no employees = Low)	

D		Analytics and Reporting			
	a. Reporting	a. The CoI programme is reported/will be reported to the board (or equivalent) NOTE: Six-monthly = High, annually = Medium, two-yearly or more = Low)			
	b. Measures/ metrics	b. Track every employee required to participate to ensure achievement of 100% compliance with CoI requirements, including submission, certification and training activities			
		c. Track conflict types and their resolution			
		d. Track understanding of CoI programme through assessment of employee interactions required to complete disclosures			
		e. Track non-disclosed employee CoIs (e.g. via social media etc.)			

E		Technology			
	1. Disclosure communications	a. All affected and relevant employees are able to make an interim disclosure of a CoI (such as that arising from a new personal or professional relationship)			
	2. CoI event management including assessment and escalation	b. All CoI events/issues are able to be recorded and managed to resolution including structured assessment and escalation			

F		Considerations			
	1. 'How far would you go?'	a. Many CoIs are purposely disguised – often via spouses and/or companies registered at the employee's home. Would your organisation proactively undertake due diligence on such issues?			

CoI Programme Performance and Risk Measures	Actual			
	Percentage			

Appendix 7:

The Telegraph

Compliance and science

A company like BT has to innovate but it cannot afford to cut corners or abuse its market position. Stefan Stern meets Keith Read, whose job it is to make sure that the regulatory sky never falls in.

Sometimes you can't help feeling that we have all got a bit too good at that great British sport of beating ourselves up. Self-flagellation may offer a kind of pleasure but it distracts from some of the achievements and success stories.

Take the tricky business of the privatisation of what was known as British Telecom before it followed convention and adopted a set of initials. While other state sell-offs may have caused anxiety and hand-wringing, BT is finally emerging, 20 years after its flotation, as a robust player in a dynamic and vigorous domestic market.

This hasn't happened by chance. Slowly, and painfully at times, the UK telecoms market has been steered by governments of both colours, and policed by a regulator who has had to grasp the various implications of dazzling new technology. The UK has led the way in this area, and its market is studied around the world as a benchmark.

Regulation and compliance have become a more important part of the lexicon of business. Many companies complain they are being suffocated by the weight of regulatory rules with the result that initiative is being stifled.

Some BT managers echo the complaints. They feel that the constant emphasis on complying with an increasingly lengthy set of rules risks making employees more cautious. One senior executive says he struggles to maintain a balance.

It has been a challenging couple of decades for the company and the search continues for the right balance.

There were run-ins aplenty with Oftel, the first regulatory body, and feisty regulators, notably Don Cruickshank, throughout the Eighties and Nineties. The most common complaint was anti-competitive behaviour and the odd grumble that the business was misusing confidential information.

Having inherited a dominant market position, BT was going to have to be heavily regulated if a healthy and competitive market were to develop. Changing the culture was a key element in the equation.

A business like BT has to innovate or die. But it cannot cut corners and abuse its market position or the regulatory sky will fall in. Just ask Microsoft about the cost of upsetting the authorities, whether in Washington or Brussels.

The man charged with leading BT's regulatory compliance is Keith Read, a seasoned professional who has spent most of his career at the firm. Earlier this month Mr Read won the Compliance Register's annual award (the industry Oscars) as the leading compliance expert in the sector. BT won the telecoms industry award as well.

Not that the success has gone to his head, or distracted Mr Read from the realities of his task. "Compliance is not always the most riveting subject," he says. "People are not knocking on my door saying 'Send us more compliance information, Keith, let us have it!' Of course, if they didn't get their pay slip they'd be all over me like a rash."

That last point is not a frivolous one. Abuse of competition law can leave a company liable for a fine of up to 10pc of turnover. For BT, with sales of £19billion, this would mean a fine of almost £2billion. "We don't need that," Mr Read says emphatically.

With the launch of Ofcom in 2003, a super-regulator now responsible for the telecoms, television, radio and wireless industries, BT had to sharpen up its act. Mr Read was appointed around that time to do just that.

"I think the company asked me to take this on for three reasons," he explains. "One was that they needed someone who knew their way round the telecoms industry. They also wanted somebody who knew their way round BT, and, perhaps most of all, they wanted somebody who was going to change things. I've been in BT a long while. I'm known for changing things and not being afraid of changing things."

One of Mr Read's previous 'mission impossible' challenges was to get a grip on BT's failing pay phones at the end of the 1980s. The firm had been stung into action in part by newspaper headlines declaring that only four in ten pay phones in an average high street were "serviceable".

Mr Read set himself three main goals in his new job. He wanted to establish a 'compliance culture' in the business, ensure relations with the regulator were good, and create better links across the industry sector.

"In the past there were sometimes concerns about how BT responded to questions from the regulator," he says. "The words used might have been 'slow' or 'incomplete'." But using BT's new 'gatekeeper' software, the company tracks its responses much more closely. It is designed not only to ensure a prompt response, but to make sure that no problems fall between the cracks of different parts of the company. While the workforce has shrunk since privatisation, BT still has just over 100,000 employees.

Compliance covers everything the business does, ranging from a field engineer turning up to keep an appointment, to call centre staff, through to a senior manager who works at headquarters.

"Or it could be a general manager in BT wholesale," Mr Read says, "who might be selling a big deal for £10m of equipment. You have to make sure that everything you do meets the rules and the requirements, not only the letter but the spirit of them."

BT staff must not abuse any customer information they may have acquired from another part of the business. They must not denigrate other service providers. Their pricing has to be clear. There are any number of potential areas where staff could find themselves tripping up.

Every BT manager has to complete five computer-based training courses over a two-year period. Non-managers have to complete one, which is a shortened composite version of the managers' five courses.

"We run 250,000 course completions every two years," Mr Read says.

"It's pass or fail. At the end of the course you have to answer a series of questions, and if you don't pass you have to keep repeating that." Not only does this become a disciplinary matter if compliance tests are not passed, but career advancement at the firm will soon depend on having reached satisfactory proficiency in compliance issues.

But establishing this 'compliance culture' has required an imaginative and multi-faceted approach. "It has to go beyond the compliance department, it is everybody's job," Mr Read says. "For some people this touches them only lightly, while for others, everything they do is about compliance – call centre staff, senior sales people, senior managers, engineers.

"You've got to get it under peoples' skin so they understand it to a level that is appropriate to their role and their job," Mr Read says. "But it's no good just throwing stuff at people, sending them 50 emails, they'll just delete them."

BT has a hotline that employees can ring for help if they think they are in danger of infringing on a compliance issue. This service has even been used on one occasion by the partner of a BT employee, who was worried that "a line was being crossed".

The BT intranet also offers the delightful 'Veronica', the virtual regulatory compliance assistant. There are a dozen 6ft-high cardboard Veronicas often to be spotted at various BT buildings around the country, and with the Christmas party season coming up it's clear that these Veronicas may be put to good use. This is just another way that BT has tried to make the compliance issue come alive for staff. "You have to be dogged and you have to be persistent, and you have to make sure people understand," Mr Read says.

"You have to make sure that if people haven't listened the first time they listen the second. And this is a continuous piece of work," he adds. "Legislation changes. It's not just at home. We have to comply wherever we are in the world, whatever the jurisdiction."

The regulator has noticed BT's efforts. "Ofcom has experienced a substantial reduction in its case load relative to Oftel," it declared last year. "This is due to a wide variety of factors, including improving relationships between stakeholders, particularly the effort BT makes to avoid unnecessary disputes."

The UK Compliance Institute has said: "There exists within BT a secure and well-functioning compliance culture such as some companies within the financial services sector would be pleased to enjoy."

Notes, Links, References & Sources

I acknowledge the wide range of wonderful articles, analyses, reports and books that I have read over some 25 years of my compliance and ethics journey, and can only express my gratitude and thanks to all their authors.

Images
VeRoniCA image courtesy of:
British Telecom (BT)
https://www.bt.com/

'Take your litter home' sign image courtesy of:
Courtesy of Tonbridge & Malling Borough Council/Lunatic Laboratories

Conflicts of Interest matrix approach courtesy of:
National Audit Office (UK)
https://www.nao.org.uk/

Links

Transparency International
https://www.transparency.org/

Global Business Ethics Survey (GBES)
https://www.ethics.org/global-business-ethics-survey/

Conflicts of Interest (CoI) – Programme Performance and Risk Assessment Questionnaire (Appendix 6)
Sources used include PwC
https://www.pwc.com/

Institute of Business Ethics (IBE)
https://www.ibe.org.uk/

References and Sources (including articles originally written by the author)
Compliance and Science
https://www.telegraph.co.uk/finance/2926767/Compliance-and-science.html

'The reality of compliance'
Police 'failed to protect murdered couple'
https://www.theguardian.com/uk/2008/feb/22/ukcrime1
Murder by the Sea
https://www.mirror.co.uk/news/uk-news/murder-sea-revenge-slaying-innocent-12660603

10 Challenges Facing Ethics and Compliance Executives
Courtesy of Syntrio Lighthouse
https://www.lighthouse-services.com/newsletters/10-challenges-facing-ethics-and-compliance-executives/

Retaliation on the Rise; How Should Companies Respond? – Timothy J. Lindon
Courtesy of Timothy J. Lindon/New York University School of Law
Program on Corporate Compliance and Enforcement at New York University School of Law
https://wp.nyu.edu/compliance_enforcement/2018/04/11/retaliation-on-the-rise-how-should-companies-respond/

"Benchmark Study Finds that 34% of Employees in the U.S. Do Not Speak Up Because of Fear of Retribution"
Courtesy of DecisionWise
https://decision-wise.com/decisionwise-benchmark-study/

The State of Ethics & Compliance in the Workplace: Global Business Ethics Survey (GBES)
"Retaliation happens quickly: 72% of employees who experienced retaliation said that it occurred within three weeks of their initial report"
Courtesy of ECI (Ethics & Compliance Initiative)
https://www.ethics.org/knowledge-center/2018-gbes-2/

US Equal Employment Opportunity Commission (EEOC)
https://www.eeoc.gov/
2021 EEOC Charge Statistics: Retaliation & Impact of Remote Work
Courtesy of Jeffrey C. Miller/BMD
https://www.bmdllc.com/resources/blog/2021-eeoc-charge-statistics-retaliation-impact-of-remote-work/

Witnessing workplace harassment and discrimination
Courtesy of Talk to Spot
https://talktospot.com/resources/resources-witness.html

How a Speak-Up Culture Can Help You Mitigate Risk
Courtesy of OneTrust/Convercent (original article partly by the author)
https://www.onetrust.com/blog/how-a-speak-up-culture-can-help-you-mitigate-risk/

Compliance and the Art of Persuasion
Courtesy of Mark Dorosz/Society of Corporate Compliance & Ethics (SCCE)/The Compliance & Ethics Blog
https://www.complianceandethics.org/compliance-and-the-art-of-persuasion/

Throw Out Your Assumptions About Whistleblowing
Courtesy of Kyle Welch/Stephen Stubben/Harvard Business Review (HBR)
https://hbr.org/2020/01/throw-out-your-assumptions-about-whistleblowing

The Science of Persuasion – Seven Principles of Persuasion
Courtesy of Dr Robert Cialdini/Influence at Work
https://www.influenceatwork.com/7-principles-of-persuasion/
Compliance Training & Employee Engagement
Courtesy of OneTrust (some original articles partly by the author)
https://www.convercent.com/blog/topic/compliance-training-employee-engagement

British Airways fine for price fixing halved
Courtesy of London Evening Standard
https://www.standard.co.uk/business/business-news/british-airways-fine-for-price-fixing-halved-7660475.html

The Challenge of Third-Party Compliance Management
Courtesy of Infosecurity
https://www.infosecurity-magazine.com/blogs/third-party-compliance-management/

Third-Party Risk Management and Due Diligence
Courtesy of OneTrust/Convercent
https://www.convercent.com/products/third-party-risk-management-and-due-diligence

Conflicts of Interest Topic Guide
Courtesy of Transparency International
https://knowledgehub.transparency.org/assets/uploads/kproducts/Topic_Guide_Conflicts_of_Interest.pdf

10 Ways to Reduce Bribery & Corruption Risks
Courtesy of Vivek Dodd/ Skillcast
https://www.skillcast.com/blog/reduce-bribery-corruption-risks

Technology Acceptance Model (TAM) – (e.g. Compliance & Ethics Acceptance Model)
Courtesy of Wikipedia
https://en.wikipedia.org/wiki/Technology_acceptance_model

Disclosures: Going on the Offensive to Mitigate Risk
Courtesy of OneTrust/Convercent (original article by the author)
https://www.onetrust.com/blog/disclosures-going-on-the-offensive-to-mitigate-risk/
https://www.convercent.com/blog/gifts-travel-entertainment-disclosures-proactively-mitigating-risk

Works Councils
Courtesy of Eurofound
www.eurofound.europa.eu

Acknowledgements

Whilst I've spent something like 25 years writing articles, papers and whitepapers on compliance, ethics, whistleblowing and a wide range of related subjects, it's a different matter to write your first book, as I have now discovered!

I would like to particularly thank my family for their love and support in my personal and professional life that brought me to this point. Without you, none of it would have been possible and I am eternally grateful. My sincere thanks also go to my wider family and friends who have supported me throughout.

I would also like to thank the many colleagues and clients who have supported me and given me opportunities in my post-British Telecom life, a hugely rewarding second career that I never expected.

Over those years, many people have given me their personal and professional support, advice, thoughts, expertise and their friendship over the years of my 'compliance journey'. I cannot mention everyone individually, but I am eternally grateful to you all; without you, this book would not have been possible.

My thanks go to two key people who made this book possible; Matt Kelly, Editor of Radical Compliance, who despite his multitude of other commitments did an outstanding job on the Foreword for me, and Dan Bernard at Tricorn Books whose experience, help and support was crucial in getting me to publication!

Lastly, I would also like to thank Graham Sheppard at British Telecom (BT), who was taken far too early but first gave me the opportunity to become the company's Deputy Director of Regulatory Compliance and started me on this journey. I will always be grateful to you, Graham.

About the Author

Keith Read is an award-winning thought leader and expert in compliance, ethics, risk and governance and was formerly the Group Compliance and Ethics Director for British Telecom (BT).

After leaving BT in 2011, he established his own boutique advisory company with a diverse range of clients, including LRN and Convercent (now OneTrust).

He is a past winner of the Compliance Register's Best Compliance Officer award when he also won the Best Compliance Company award for BT. He was subsequently the subject of a full-page Daily Telegraph national press article – 'Compliance and Science' (Appendices)

He has an innovative and practical approach to compliance, using techniques such as Compliance not Complacence whilst recognising the Cost of Compliance. His thought-provoking ideas and infectious enthusiasm appeal to diverse compliance, ethics and governance audiences, and readers, worldwide.

Index

A

Analytics 42, 80, 150
Anti-bribery 14, 85, 91-2, 110 135, 149, 150, 159
Anti-retaliation 156, 157, 158, 159
Anti-Trust 155
Assessment 6, 150, 169, 179
Audit 74, 150, 178
Awareness 44-5, 68-9, 72, 74, 81, 89, 92, 154, 160, 170, 179

B

Branding 42, 72, 100, 154

C

Code of Conduct 45, 73, 154, 156
Communications 149, 154
Competition Law 85, 95, 118, 149, 177
Competitions 5, 116
Compliance and Ethics Covenant 27, 32, 35, 36, 37, 38
Compliance and Ethics Passport 25, 26, 27, 28, 29
Conflicts of Interest 5, 6, 17, 86, 92, 93, 103, 104, 106, 107, 108, 109, 110, 111, 124, 128, 131, 133, 134, 146, 152, 154, 169, 178, 179, 181
Contractors 13, 17, 22, 30, 33, 40, 66, 74, 76, 101, 148, 154
Corruption 6, 85, 91, 92, 110, 135, 137, 149, 150, 153, 154, 181
Cost of compliance 18, 94-7, 128, 145

D

Data privacy 167-8
Data protection 150, 154
Data retention 61, 108
Dawn raids 119, 128, 150, 152-3 145
Declaration 21, 24, 90, 173
Demonstrable compliance 19, 23, 26
Disclosure 17, 62-3, 85, 90, 92, 103-10, 116, 131, 134, 146, 149, 150, 159, 167, 172-5
Disparate 125, 129

E

Education 14, 17, 22, 32, 98, 113, 135, 146, 174
Employees 107, 179
Escalation /escalations 21-2, 25, 43, 104, 109, 143, 166, 174-5

Ethics 5, 6, 13, 24, 25, 26, 27, 28, 29, 32, 34, 35, 36, 37, 38, 61, 79, 83, 88, 94, 98, 112, 113, 114, 115, 116, 117, 118, 119, 123, 127, 142, 152, 154, 179, 180, 181, 183, 184, 185, 186

EU Whistleblower Protection Directive 5, 6, 30, 55, 63, 64, 65, 66, 67, 75, 77, 79, 80, 150, 153, 154, 156, 157, 159, 168, 169

F

Feedback 19, 43, 69, 104, 110, 116-7, 152, 163, 166
Fraud 139

G

General Data Protection Regulation 61, 64, 166, 184
Governance 13, 107

H

Hotlines and helplines 39
How far would you go 5, 88, 185
Human resources 185
Hygiene factors 108

I

Identity cards 73
Input (measures of compliance) 185
Insights 19, 70, 108-9, 113-6, 125-6

J

Jackets (hi-visibility – predictive measurement) 124

K

Killing – compliance & ethics case example 13

L

Lanyards 73, 185
Legal/legality 10, 17, 21, 39, 64-9, 73-6, 93, 96, 100, 104, 110, 113, 155, 167, 171
Lessons 23, 129, 162
Lessons (compliance & ethics) 16

M

Measures 124, 185
Mirror (and windscreen/windshield 53, 59, 68, 80, 114, 124, 128
Mock dawn raids 150, 152, 155
Multiplier (retaliation) 78

N

Nudge 5, 98

O

Output (measures of compliance & ethics) 22, 60, 91, 124-5

P

Passcards (identity cards) 45, 73
Passport 5, 25, 26, 27, 28, 29, 178, 184, 185
Perverse incentives 115, 136, 139
Policy 21, 52-3, 63-6, 80, 108, 116, 124, 128, 134, 136, 150, 151-7, 168, 173
Posters 44, 50, 72, 74, 118

Q

Questions and answers (typical) – works councils 162

R

Reporting (whistleblowing) 22, 32, 41-2, 44-6, 49, 50, 61, 66, 68, 70, 72-6, 81-2, 1000, 104, 109, 110, 111, 126, 130, 138, 152, 158, 166, 174
Restaurant (staff) 32, 45, 50, 71-3, 119, 136
Retaliation 5, 6, 52, 55, 63, 64, 67, 78, 79, 80, 150, 156, 158, 179, 180, 185
Retaliation Reverse Burden of Proof 63-7, 80, 159
Retention (data) 61, 72, 108, 116
Risk and risk management 14, 30, 146, 149, 162

S

Saw-tooth (pattern of Compliance & Ethics) 94, 143
Scores on the Doors 5, 30, 32, 33, 34, 178, 186
Senior management – influencing 10, 32, 36, 74, 104, 120, 147
Sludge 5, 98, 99
Stakeholder/stakeholder management 100

T

Telephone training 102
Testing – whistleblowing 29, 32, 48, 82, 127-8, 134
Text (SMS) 17, 22, 99
Third party 31, 66
Third-Party Risk Management (TPRM) 30, 150
Tipping Point – bribery 28, 125-6, 135-8
Training 25, 36, 98, 149, 180

U

Unconventional 5, 94

V

VeRoniCA 5, 39, 42, 43, 44, 72, 100, 178
Virtual Regulatory Compliance Assistant 42, 72, 100

W

Whistleblower Protection Directive (EU)
Whistleblowing 161-9 170 178 179
Wider Workforce (Reaching) 22, 44
Work-based relationship 17, 22, 74, 146, 157-9
Works councils 131, 132, 155

Y

Yawing (Saw-tooth (pattern of Compliance & Ethics) 143

Z

Z - Card 45, 73